Heracles Gods and goddesses have all the fun, but a hero's work is never done.

Heracles Wanted: Handyman to Help Hero with Chores

 Hecatoncheires
Did somebody call a HANDyman? We've got hundreds!

 Atlas
I'd help you, buddy, but I've got my hands full.

 Midas
I'll hold that for you. *Oops* … my bad.

 Echo
OOPS! OOPS! OOPS! OOPS! OOPS! OOPS! OOPS! OOPS! OOPS! OOPS! …

 Narcissus
Who *are* you?

Satyrs
Work, work, work. Work is for suckers.
We want to play!

Persephone
Let's play hide-and-seek. I'll go first.

Prophets
We see you!

Odysseus
We can hide in this wooden horse.

Oedipus
You'll ruin the surprise.

Hera
HERACLES! You can play when your chores
are done ... which means never!

CONTENT CONSULTANT
William Hansen
Professor Emeritus of Classical Studies and Folklore
Indiana University, Bloomington

Library of Congress Cataloging-in-Publication Data
Otfinoski, Steven.
All in the family: a look-it-up guide to the in-laws, outlaws, and
offspring of mythology / Steven Otfinoski.
p. cm. -- (Mythlopedia)
Includes bibliographical references and index.
ISBN-13: 978-1-60631-025-0 (lib. bdg.) 978-1-60631-057-1 (pbk.)
ISBN-10: 1-60631-025-9 (lib. bdg.) 1-60631-057-7 (pbk.)
1. Mythology, Greek--Encyclopedias, Juvenile. 2.
Heroes--Mythology--Greece--Encyclopedias, Juvenile. I. Title.
BL795.H46O38 2009
398.20938'03--dc22
                                                        2009020999

6 7 8 9 10 R 18 17 16 15 14 13   62

MYTHLOPEDIA

ALL IN The FAMILY

Can I get a little help here?

A Look-It-Up Guide to the In-laws, Outlaws, and Offspring of Mythology

STEVEN OTFINOSKI

SCHOLASTIC

ALL IN THE FAMILY

OUCH!

Achilles

PROFILES AND MYTHS
Up close and personal with the gods of the pantheon

Apollo

A little down
and to the left ...

Thanks, Apollo!

Paris

TMI

THE MYTHLOPEDIA INTRODUCTION

Are you ready to get your myth on? Then you've come to the right place: MYTHLOPEDIA, your one-stop shop for everything you need to know about the stars of Greek mythology. From gods and monsters to goddesses and heroes, the myths that rocked the ancient world are ready to rock yours—if you're ready to read on! But first, check out a little background info that will help you make sense of these amazing characters and stories.

So, what is mythology?

Good question! "Mythology" is the word used to describe all the myths of a particular society. People who specialize in studying myths are called "mythologists." From the Yoruba of West Africa to the Inca of South America, from the Norse of Europe to the Navajo of North America, every culture has its own myths that help us understand its customs and ways of viewing the world.

What is a myth?

Simply put, a myth is a kind of story. But not just any old story! Most myths have one or more of these characteristics:

- Myths are usually about gods, goddesses, or supernatural beings with greater powers and abilities than ordinary humans.

- Myths explain the origins of the world or how human customs came to be.

- Myths take place in a time long, long ago, usually in the earliest days of humanity (or just before humans showed up on Earth).

- Myths were usually thought to be true by their original tellers—no matter how wild or strange they seem to us.

TWO NAMES, POWERS THE SAME

Many gods and goddesses have both Greek and Roman names. That's because the ancient Romans adopted a great deal of Greek mythology and made it their own. Generally, that deity's powers and myths stayed the same— even though he or she had a new name. As a result, the study of Greek and Roman mythology is often grouped together under the name "classical mythology."

What is the purpose of myths?

A better question might be: What *isn't* the purpose of myths? Myths can:

➤ explain how things came to be—like the origin of the universe or the creation of humans;

➤ teach people about the values and beliefs that are important in their society; and

➤ contain deep religious significance to the people who tell and believe in them.

Perhaps most importantly, studying myths can teach us about people around the world—their cultures and what is (or was) important to them.

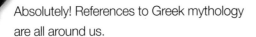

Do myths really matter today? After all, mortals have reality TV.

Absolutely! References to Greek mythology are all around us.

➤ Ever heard of Nike brand athletic gear? Meet Nike, personification and goddess of victory.

➤ What would Valentine's Day be without the god of love, Cupid—or Eros, as the ancient Greeks called him?

➤ Does *Apollo 13* ring a bell? The first crewed U.S. space missions were named for Apollo, the god of archery and prophecy.

Bottom line: References to ancient myths are everywhere, from science to pop culture, and knowing about them will help you understand more about the world we live in.

HOW DID WE LEARN THESE STORIES?

At first, Greek mythology was passed along orally through storytelling, songs, and poetry. We learned the stories from written versions, such as Homer's epic poems *The Iliad* and *The Odyssey*, which tell about the great deeds of heroes. Other sources are Hesiod's *Theogony*, which describes the origins of the world and the gods, and the *Homeric Hymns*, a collection of poems addressed to different gods.

ATF

ALL IN THE FAMILY

What was a typical day like for the heroes and mortals of Greek myth? In a word: exhausting! A famous hero battled monsters of all shapes and sizes but was done in by an uncomfortable shirt. The Trojan War lasted for ten years and brought out the best—and worst—in everybody. And the first female may have been gifted but she caused a heap of trouble.

These characters were the offspring of the gods and goddesses of Greek mythology. Many had one divine and one mortal parent. So they had unusual—sometimes superhuman—qualities, but they couldn't live forever (only deities were **immortal**). Some of these heroes may have been real, although it's unlikely they rode flying horses or turned everything they touched to gold. Their thrilling adventures have inspired writers and artists for hundreds of years.

We could go on and on but as any hero will tell you, actions speak louder than words. So let's get to the good stuff. You're about to meet some of the superstars of Greek mythology!

Heracles Let's just keep this …

ALL IN THE FAMILY!

Profile of Achilles

Sounds Like: **uh-kil'-eez**

Generation: ☐ Titan
☐ Olympian
☑ Other: Hero

Characteristics: Courage
Invincibility (almost)
Moodiness

Attributes: Armor
Sword

Top 10 Things to Know About Me:

10. My mom tried to make me immortal—
    she should have double-dipped.

9. There's a tendon in the ankle named
   for me.

8. I'm not a team player, especially when
   I've been crossed.

7. I let my best friend, Patroclus, borrow my
   armor but it couldn't save him.

6. I'm nearly invincible—except for one little
   spot. Thanks, Mom. *Not!*

5. I've got friends in high places.

4. When Agamemnon took my girl, I
   pouted—big time.

3. I killed the Trojan hero Hector and
   returned his body to his grieving
   dad.

2. I'm the star of an epic, Homer's
   The Iliad. Autographs, anyone?

1. That wimp Paris killed me with
   an arrow that hit me in the
   guess-where.

Ouch!

Family, Flings, Friends, and Foes

▼ Parents

**Peleus and
Thetis**

▼ Offspring

Pyrrhus

▼ Flings

Deïdamia

Briseis

Polyxena

▼ Friends

Odysseus

Patroclus

Hephaestus

ACHILLES

A REAL HEEL

I QUIT! I never wanted to fight in that stupid Trojan War anyway. Now that Agamemnon has stolen my best girl, I'm out. So what if Briseis was a prisoner—she was *my* prisoner! I'd like to see how the Greeks do without me. Nobody else is as brave, strong, or fierce as I am. I'm practically *invincible*! When my mom convinces Zeus to back the Trojans, they'll see how wrong they were. Agamemnon will *beg* me to fight with him—again!

REALITY CHECK

It isn't every hero who has a body part named for him. The Achilles tendon is at the back of the ankle and attaches the calf muscle to the heel bone. It is the toughest and strongest tendon in the human body.

Want to know more? Go to: http://www.achillestendon.com/

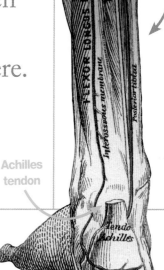

Achilles tendon

▼ Foes

Agamemnon

Hector

Paris

ACHILLES

Αχιλλευς

"Hit me with your best shot."

MYTHLOPEDIA

IT'S GREEK TO ME

The legendary Trojan War was fought between the Greeks and the Trojans at the city of Troy. It all started when Paris, prince of Troy, kidnapped Helen, the most beautiful woman in the world and the wife of King Menelaus of Sparta.

Armies from many kingdoms of southern Greece went to war to win Helen back. Among the leaders were Menelaus's brother Agamemnon, Achilles, and Odysseus. Setting out in more than a thousand ships, the Greek armies sailed across the Aegean Sea. The Greeks laid siege to Troy for ten years, finally taking the city by surprise and trickery—in the form of a wooden horse.

By the way, that's why they say of Helen that her face launched a thousand ships.

A HERO IS MADE, NOT BORN

A hero's mom leaves her mark.

Achilles, the handsomest and bravest of the Greek warriors, was the son of Peleus, king of Phthiotis, and Thetis, a sea **nymph**. Soon after Achilles was born, his mother took him to the River Styx, whose waters were known for their magical powers. Thetis dipped Achilles' entire body into the water, making him **invincible**. His entire body? Well, not quite. Thetis didn't want her baby to drown, so she held on tight to one of his heels as she dunked him in the river. And invincible? Not exactly invincible, either. The spot on his heel where his mother held him became Achilles' one **vulnerable** spot.

Thetis

Baby Achilles

HIDING IN PLAIN SIGHT

Achilles acts like a man and gives himself away.

Achilles' mother, Thetis, had a **premonition** that Achilles would die at Troy. So when the war began, she dressed her son as a woman and hid him among the ladies in the court of King Lycomedes. Odysseus, a Greek general, came searching for the legendary hero. Suspecting that Achilles was hiding among the women, Odysseus displayed a collection of weapons and armor before them. Achilles' eyes shone as he gazed at the swords and shields—and Odysseus had his man.

Achilles

ACHILLES WON'T FIGHT

A hero sulks, loses a friend, and a prophecy is fulfilled.

After ten years of fighting in the Trojan War, Achilles earned a reputation as a courageous warrior. But when Agamemnon, leader of the Greek troops, ordered Achilles to hand over Briseis, a Trojan girl he had captured, Achilles **begrudgingly** complied. Then he stormed off the battlefield and refused to fight. Sulking in his tent, Achilles asked his mother to persuade the mighty god Zeus to aid the Trojans, to show the Greeks how much they needed him. With Zeus on their side, the Trojans handed the Greeks many defeats.

Agamemnon begged Achilles to get back in the fight, even promising to return Briseis, but Achilles refused. Finally Achilles' best friend, Patroclus, borrowed the sulking hero's armor and **chariot** and joined the battle. There he was killed by the Trojan leader— and Paris's brother— Hector, who thought he had killed Achilles.

Achilles (and posse)

Achilles, devastated at the loss of his best friend, turned his rage against Hector. Driving his chariot, he chased Hector three times around Troy before killing him. Then Achilles tied Hector's lifeless body to his chariot and dragged the body around the walls of the city. Finally, at Zeus's command, Achilles returned Hector's body to his grieving father, King Priam.

But all was not well. As Hector lay dying, he had prophesied that Achilles would be killed by Paris and Apollo. Back on the battlefield, Paris sought to avenge Hector's death. He sneaked up on Achilles, took aim with his bow and arrow, and shot. With the god Apollo guiding the arrow, it struck Achilles in his one vulnerable spot—his heel. The great warrior died from a foot wound, and a **prophecy** was fulfilled.

Paris

19

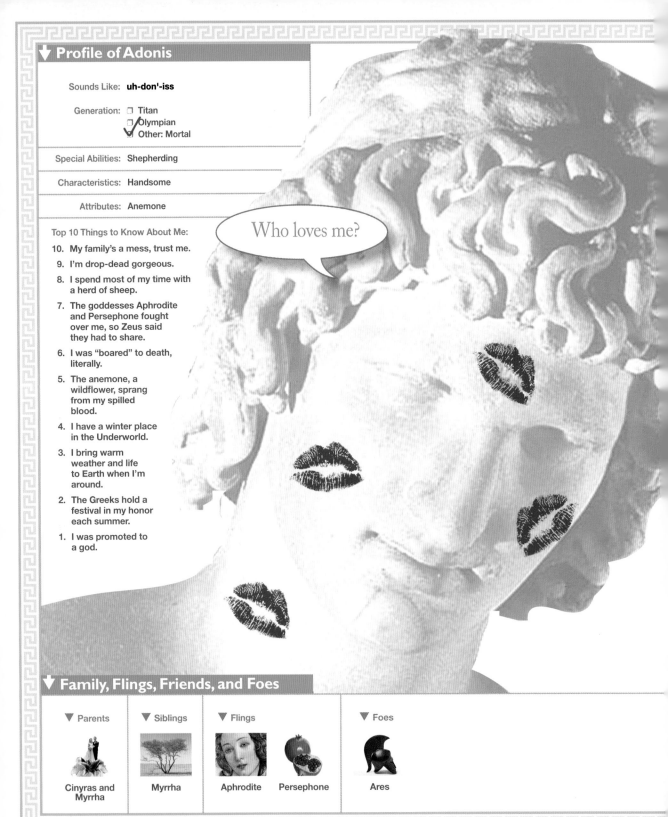

▼ Profile of Adonis

Sounds Like: uh-don'-iss

Generation: ☐ Titan
☐ Olympian
☑ Other: Mortal

Special Abilities: Shepherding

Characteristics: Handsome

Attributes: Anemone

Top 10 Things to Know About Me:

10. My family's a mess, trust me.

9. I'm drop-dead gorgeous.

8. I spend most of my time with a herd of sheep.

7. The goddesses Aphrodite and Persephone fought over me, so Zeus said they had to share.

6. I was "boared" to death, literally.

5. The anemone, a wildflower, sprang from my spilled blood.

4. I have a winter place in the Underworld.

3. I bring warm weather and life to Earth when I'm around.

2. The Greeks hold a festival in my honor each summer.

1. I was promoted to a god.

Who loves me?

▼ Family, Flings, Friends, and Foes

▼ Parents	▼ Siblings	▼ Flings		▼ Foes
Cinyras and Myrrha	Myrrha	Aphrodite	Persephone	Ares

ADONIS
OLYMPIAN HUNK

It's not easy being the most handsome man alive. Sure, there are perks to having naturally curly hair, a face that makes the ladies swoon, and the body of a god. I'll admit I was flattered when Aphrodite and Persephone fought over me. But beauty has a dark side. I've been locked in a chest, held captive in the Underworld, and even attacked by a god disguised as a boar! Oh, to be a simple shepherd again—but even the sheep can't protect me from my admirers!

REALITY CHECK

The flower associated with Adonis, the anemone, gets its name from a Greek word that means "windflower" in English. The anemone has a fragile flower that blows open in the wind, then blows away as it dies.

Want to know more? Go to: http://www.plantingflower-bulbs.com/anemone-flowers.htm

The boy is mine!

Yoo-hoo, Adonis!

Persephone

Aphrodite

21

Αδωνις

ADONIS

"Hello, gorgeous!"

MYTHLOPEDIA

IT'S GREEK TO ME

Adonis is a vegetation god. His birth and death relate to the agricultural calendar. In ancient Greece, during the Festival of Adonis, women would plant herb gardens known as gardens of Adonis. The plants would quickly grow, then die, mirroring Adonis's short life.

ADORABLE ADONIS

A cute baby causes a big problem.

Adonis was a handsome young shepherd. He was the offspring of King Cinyras of Cyprus and his daughter Myrrha (Smyrna). When the king discovered that the mother of his son was his daughter, he threatened to kill her. Myrrha pleaded with the gods to protect her, and the mighty god Zeus **transformed** the girl into a tree, called myrrh, which is said to weep tears (it's really sap). In time, their baby, Adonis, burst forth from the tree.

Adonis was so beautiful that the goddess of love, Aphrodite, fell in love with him. To hide him from the other gods, she locked him in a trunk and left him to be cared for by Persephone, the queen of the **Underworld**. Persephone also fell in love with the adorable boy and refused to return him to Aphrodite. So the lovestruck goddesses pleaded with the mighty Zeus to **intervene**.

Zeus decided that the goddesses should share the boy for eternity. Adonis was to spend one third of the year with Aphrodite, one third with Persephone, and he could do what he wished with the third part, so he chose to spend it with Aphrodite.

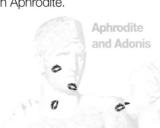

Aphrodite and Adonis

HUNTING ACCIDENT

Adonis goes hunting and is "boared" to death.

Adonis grew into a handsome youth. He and Aphrodite spent hours together on Earth, cuddling, hunting, and cuddling some more. One day, while hunting, Adonis wounded a wild boar. The boar then turned on Adonis and killed him. Adonis died in Aphrodite's arms. Where his blood fell to the ground, fragile wildflowers, called anemones, sprang up.

There are several versions of this myth. Some stories say that the wild boar was sent by the jealous god of war, Ares, who loved Aphrodite. Other versions say Ares transformed himself into the boar to kill Adonis. And still others say the boar was sent by Artemis, the goddess of hunting.

The story of Adonis is one version of the myth of death in winter and rebirth in spring or summer. When Adonis is with Aphrodite, it is spring and summer; flowers bloom and plants grow in abundance. When he is with Persephone, in fall and winter, plants die and the earth is barren.

Adonis

Aphrodite

Are you friendly?

Adonis

FROM THE DESK OF APHRODITE

Dearest Adonis,
Miss you desperately.
So does all the earth.
See you in the spring.
Your goddess of love,
Aphrodite
xoxoxo

REALITY CHECK

English poet Percy Bysshe Shelley wrote his elegy "Adonais" (Adonis) to fellow poet John Keats after Keats's early death in 1821.

Want to know more? Go to: http://poetryfoundation.org/

wild thing

Profile of Agamemnon

Sounds Like: ag-uh-mem'-nahn

Generation:
☐ Titan
☐ Olympian
☑ Other: Hero

Characteristics: Arrogance
Majesty
Leadership
Selfishness

It's always bad news with you, Cassandra.

Top 10 Things to Know About Me:

10. I am the king of Mycenae.

9. I led the Greeks in the Trojan War.

8. I offended Artemis—that goddess doesn't get mad, she gets even!

7. I tried to steal Achilles' girl. Man, that guy can pout.

6. I made the mistake of taking my girlfriend home to meet my wife.

5. I made Apollo really mad—and now I don't feel so good.

4. Next time I'll run the other way when Clytemnestra offers to run me a bath.

3. My kids Orestes and Electra had my back, but Orestes paid the price.

2. I shouldn't have ignored the advice of a prophet.

1. You can read all about me in Homer's *The Iliad*.

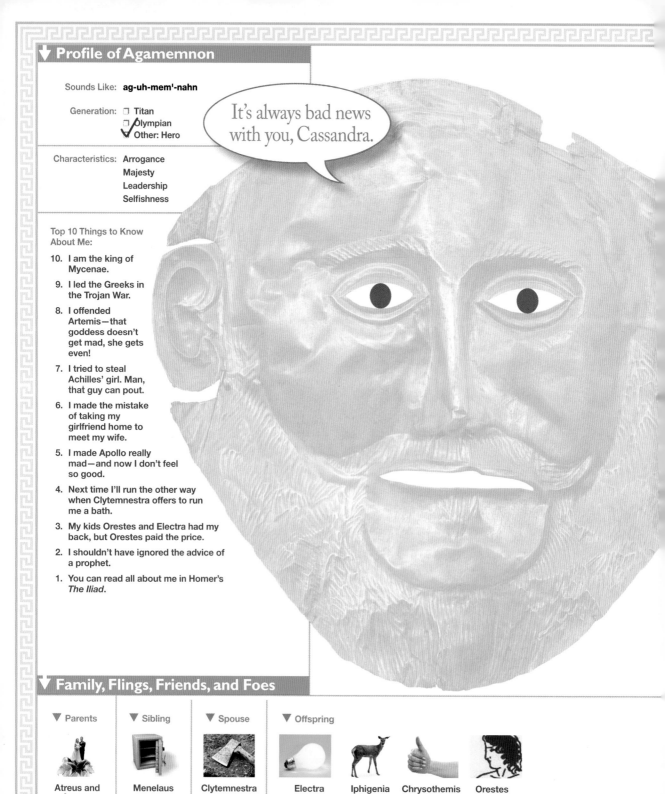

Family, Flings, Friends, and Foes

▼ Parents	▼ Sibling	▼ Spouse	▼ Offspring			
Atreus and Aerope	Menelaus	Clytemnestra	Electra	Iphigenia	Chrysothemis	Orestes

AGAMEMNON

HAPPY HOMECOMING

Dear Clytemnestra,

The wind's finally blowing again—I'll be home soon! So much has happened in these ten years! Turns out, your sister Helen is quite the troublemaker. Please don't kill me, but I'm bringing my, *ahem*, friend Cassandra with me. Funny, she keeps telling me I shouldn't go home. By the way, we had a close call with our Iphigenia—will give you the details when I get there. Can't wait to see you. I'm dying for a hot bath!

Love,
Agamemnon

REALITY CHECK

The so-called Mask of Agamemnon was discovered by **archeologist** Heinrich Schliemann at the ancient site of Mycenae in 1876. Schliemann believed it had once covered the face of Agamemnon, Mycenae's most legendary king. The mask has since been dated to about 1500 BCE, a full three hundred years before Agamemnon would have lived, had he been a real person.

Want to know more? Go to: http://proteus.brown.edu/greekpast/4917

> I wouldn't go home if I were you.

Cassandra

▼ Flings

Chryseis

Cassandra

▼ Foes

Artemis

Aegisthus

Achilles

AGAMEMNON

"I'm the leader of the pack."

MYTHLOPEDIA

Αγαμεμνων

IT'S GREEK TO ME

Who was who in the Trojan War?

TEAM GREECE
Achilles—best warrior
Agamemnon—general, married to Clytemnestra
Ajax—second-best warrior
Helen—cause of the war, kidnapped by Paris
Menelaus—brother of Agamemnon, married to Helen
Odysseus—hero who came up with the idea of the Trojan Horse

TEAM TROY
Hector—number-one son and best warrior
Paris—number-two son and Helen's kidnapper
Priam—king of Troy

THIS MEANS WAR!

Kidnap a beautiful woman and trouble will follow.

Agamemnon and Menelaus were sons of King Atreus and Queen Aerope of Mycenae. Agamemnon was married to Clytemnestra, a daughter of Leda and Tyndareus. Menelaus became the king of Sparta and married Clytemnestra's sister Helen.

Helen was known as the most beautiful woman in all of Greece. In fact, the goddess Aphrodite had promised Paris, the prince of Troy, that she would make Helen fall in love with him if he picked Aphrodite as the winner in a beauty contest. So Paris chose Aphrodite as the contest winner. But rather than wait for Helen to come to him, he kidnapped Helen while her husband was away and took her to Troy. This started big trouble!

The Greeks demanded Helen's return. When the Trojans refused to give her back, Agamemnon gathered the Greek troops aboard a thousand ships and prepared to sail to Troy.

REALITY CHECK

Helen's beauty has been praised by writers and artists for centuries. In *Dr. Faustus*, by Christopher Marlowe, Faustus sees the ghost of Helen and says:

"Was this the face that launch'd a thousand ships,/and burnt the topless towers of Ilium [Troy]?"

Helen

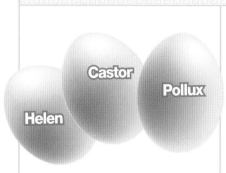
Helen · Castor · Pollux

THE BIRTH OF A BEAUTY

A queen flees a flirt and becomes a fowl.

Zeus, the mighty Olympian god who ruled heaven and earth, fell in love with Leda, the queen of Sparta and mother of Agamemnon's wife, Clytemnestra. Leda wasn't interested in an affair with the notorious ladies' man, so she **transformed** herself into many shapes and fled over land and sea. When she became a goose to avoid the god, Zeus turned himself into a swan and captured her. Not long after, Leda's children were born as eggs. When the eggs hatched, out popped the beautiful Helen, and the brothers Castor and Pollux.

A COSTLY BOAST

Agamemnon stalls on his way to Troy.

When Agamemnon gathered his troops and prepared to sail for Troy, there was just one little problem: no wind.

Earlier, while hunting, Agamemnon had shot a deer. Proud of his excellent skill with a bow and arrow, Agamemnon boasted that not even Artemis, the goddess of the hunt, could have made such a good shot. This infuriated Artemis. The goddess retaliated by refusing to allow the winds to blow and fill the sails of the Greek fleet until Agamemnon made a sacrifice to her. What was the sacrifice? His beloved daughter Iphigenia. To appease Artemis and secure a favorable wind, a grief-filled Agamemnon agreed. But at the last moment, Artemis spared the girl's life. (According to other versions, Iphigenia was killed.) The ships' sails filled with wind, and the Greeks set off for Troy.

Stop showing off!

Agamemnon

THE TROJAN WAR HIGHLIGHT REEL

- Paris kidnaps Helen, takes her to Troy
- Agamemnon leads Greek fleet to Troy
- Hero Achilles helps Greeks trounce Trojans in battles
- Achilles and Agamemnon capture two Trojan women; Agamemnon takes Chryseis; Achilles takes Briseis
- Apollo demands release of Chryseis; Agamemnon refuses; Apollo infects Greek camp with plague
- Agamemnon gives up Chryseis, takes Briseis from Achilles
- Achilles fumes and refuses to fight
- Achilles' mom urges Zeus to punish Greeks; he helps Trojans trounce Greeks
- Patroclus borrows Achilles' armor and **chariot** and is killed by Hector
- Achilles kills Hector
- Paris kills Achilles
- Greeks give Trojans a surprise gift: a wooden horse filled with Greek soldiers
- Gift is opened; Troy is sacked
- Agamemnon returns home with girlfriend Cassandra; wife, not amused, kills both

WANNA BUY A TROJAN HORSE?

It's like no other wooden horse on the road!

ROAD WARRIORS WANTED!

Built for extremes, the new off-road Trojan Horse is more compact and innovative than ever, with a convertible body design (removable side panels, emergency roof exit, kick-out doors) and detailed craftsmanship.

Emergency roof exit

FEATURES:

✓ 5-speed manual transmission for obstacle climbing—and gate-crashing
✓ Pegasus horsepower system
✓ Siren Surround-Sound radio
✓ Orion North-Star navigation system
✓ Roomy bench seating holds up to 50 soldiers in full armor
✓ Cargo space: Full trunk; cargo hold; roof rack optional

Roomy bench seating

SPECIAL OPTIONS

✓ "Surprise Factor" acoustic system
✓ Fold-down tailgate for quick load and unload
✓ "Belly-of-the-Beast" trapdoor that lets passengers out, not in
✓ Interior/exterior custom detailing

Fold-down tailgate

BE A HERO! PUT YOURSELF IN A TROJAN HORSE TODAY!

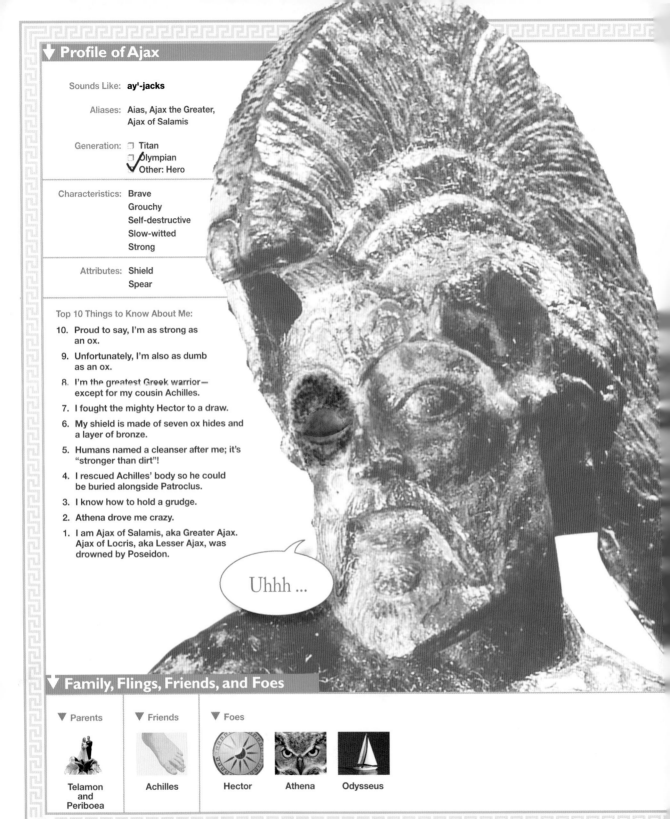

▼ Profile of Ajax

Sounds Like:	**ay'-jacks**
Aliases:	**Aias, Ajax the Greater, Ajax of Salamis**
Generation:	☐ Titan ☐ Olympian ✓ Other: Hero
Characteristics:	**Brave** **Grouchy** **Self-destructive** **Slow-witted** **Strong**
Attributes:	**Shield** **Spear**

Top 10 Things to Know About Me:

10. Proud to say, I'm as strong as an ox.

9. Unfortunately, I'm also as dumb as an ox.

8. I'm the greatest Greek warrior—except for my cousin Achilles.

7. I fought the mighty Hector to a draw.

6. My shield is made of seven ox hides and a layer of bronze.

5. Humans named a cleanser after me; it's "stronger than dirt"!

4. I rescued Achilles' body so he could be buried alongside Patroclus.

3. I know how to hold a grudge.

2. Athena drove me crazy.

1. I am Ajax of Salamis, aka Greater Ajax. Ajax of Locris, aka Lesser Ajax, was drowned by Poseidon.

Uhhh ...

▼ Family, Flings, Friends, and Foes

▼ Parents	▼ Friends	▼ Foes		
Telamon and Periboea	Achilles	Hector	Athena	Odysseus

AJAX

ALL BRAWN, NO BRAIN

Uh, lemme tell you something. Words are, uh, useless. If you have, like, the Trojan army pickin' a fight over some princess, what are you, uh, gonna do? Ask 'em to get, you know, lost? No! You, uh, you're gonna, like, fight! Right? With, um, a spear. And a, you know, sword. And, uh, armor. Yeah, armor. I, uh, ain't no brainiac but you can count on me to, uh, lead the fight. You know?

What's the matter, A? Cat got your tongue?

Odysseus

AJAX

"Are you talkin' to *ME*?"

MYTH OPEDIA

Αιας

IT'S GREEK TO ME

Two soldiers named Ajax fought for the Greeks at Troy. Ajax the Greater, from Salamis, and Ajax the Lesser, from Locris. Ajax the Lesser was known as a good fighter, but his manners were crude, to say the least. He attacked Cassandra in the goddess Athena's temple.

Not one to take such an offense lightly, Athena caused his ship to be wrecked on its way back to Greece. Poseidon, god of the seas, saved Ajax's life, but the ungrateful Greek boasted that he had saved himself. When Poseidon heard that, he dropped Ajax back into the sea, where he drowned. That's what you get when you try to upstage a god!

A FIERCE FIGHTER

A warrior wins his enemy's respect.

Ajax the Greater led the Greek troops from the island of Salamis against Troy. A giant of a man, he killed many enemy soldiers.

Ajax carried an enormous shield and spear in battle. Once he held off an entire Trojan army all by himself. He fought in hand-to-hand combat twice with the Trojan hero Hector, both times failing to finish him off. The two warriors ended up respecting each other. Hector gave Ajax his spear as a present, and Ajax gave Hector his belt.

Ajax

Hector

Hector gave
Ajax his spear

Ajax gave
Hector his belt

Athletic contest for
Achilles' armor

BATTLE FOR THE ARMOR

A tough fighter is KO'd by a smooth talker.

When the hero Patroclus was killed by Hector, Ajax bravely rescued his body from enemy territory. With the help of Odysseus, he did the same when his cousin Achilles was killed by Paris.

Afterward, both Ajax and Odysseus wanted Achilles' armor, which had been made by Hephaestus, the god of **blacksmithing**. To decide who would get it, they competed in a series of athletic contests. These physical contests ended in a tie. Next, a speaking contest was held. Odysseus spoke eloquently while poor, tongue-tied Ajax struggled to get his words out. Needless to say, Odysseus won the armor.

Ajax gets
tongue-tied

REALITY CHECK

You can see actual pieces of ancient Greek armor and weaponry at many museums around the world. New York City's Metropolitan Museum of Art's Department of Greek and Roman Art has an excellent collection, including a seventh century BCE helmet and a fourth century BCE **cuirass**.

Want to know more? Go to:
http://www.metmuseum.org/toah/hd/
gwar/hd_gwar.htm

"Those were sheep? My bad!"

SOLDIERS OR SHEEP?

Ajax loses a contest—and his mind.

When Ajax lost the speaking contest and Achilles' armor to Odysseus, he was so upset that he fell to the ground unconscious. After regaining consciousness, Ajax was out of his mind, thanks to the goddess Athena, who had favored Odysseus to win. In his dazed condition, Ajax saw a flock of sheep and thought it was an army of Greeks led by Odysseus and Agamemnon. So he attacked the flock and killed every sheep. When Ajax returned to his senses, he couldn't believe what he had done. Rather than live with the shame of his act, he threw himself on the spear Hector had given him and died.

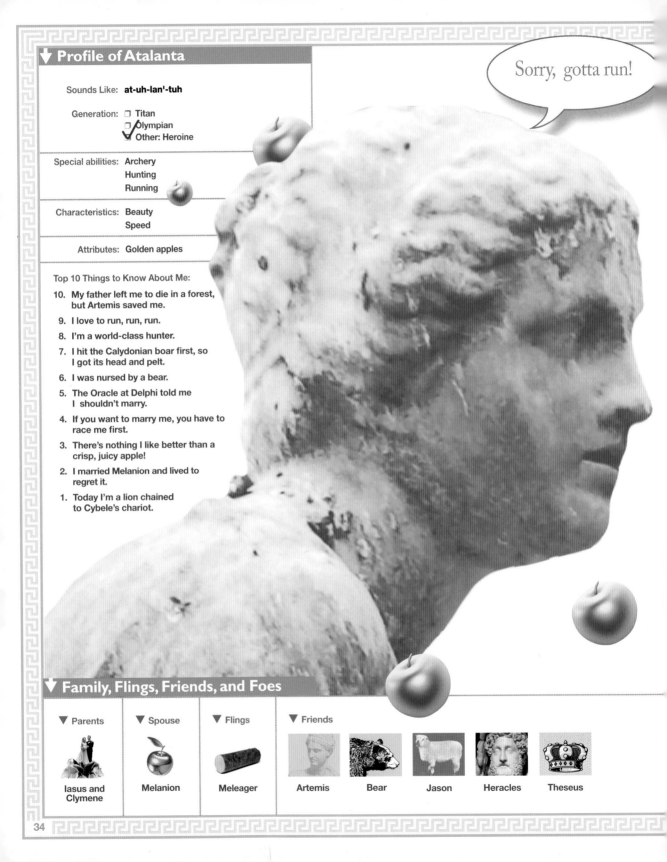

▼ Profile of Atalanta

Sounds Like: **at-uh-lan'-tuh**

Generation: ☐ Titan
☐ Olympian
☑ Other: Heroine

Special abilities: Archery
Hunting
Running

Characteristics: Beauty
Speed

Attributes: Golden apples

Top 10 Things to Know About Me:

10. My father left me to die in a forest, but Artemis saved me.

9. I love to run, run, run.

8. I'm a world-class hunter.

7. I hit the Calydonian boar first, so I got its head and pelt.

6. I was nursed by a bear.

5. The Oracle at Delphi told me I shouldn't marry.

4. If you want to marry me, you have to race me first.

3. There's nothing I like better than a crisp, juicy apple!

2. I married Melanion and lived to regret it.

1. Today I'm a lion chained to Cybele's chariot.

Sorry, gotta run!

▼ Family, Flings, Friends, and Foes

▼ Parents	▼ Spouse	▼ Flings	▼ Friends				
Iasus and Clymene	Melanion	Meleager	Artemis	Bear	Jason	Heracles	Theseus

ATALANTA

WANNA RACE?

Looking for running tips? I'm your girl. First, you need a good motivator to push through the burn, like avoiding marriage to some bum who isn't fit to lace your sandals. Ever since I started racing those love-struck losers, I've improved my overall time by 50 percent! Second, don't stop for any golden apples. They can really slow you down. Finally, keep a supply of darts handy to kill the competition.

Care for a juicy apple?

Melanion

▼ Foes

Cybele

Boar

ATALANTA

"I'm the original runaway bride!"

MYTHLOPEDIA

Ατaλaντη

IT'S GREEK TO ME

Ancient Greeks believed that the gods spoke to mortals through **oracles**. A **mortal** could ask a question of an oracle, who would communicate the god's response. The word *oracle* was also used for the response itself as well as the place where the communication happened. Apollo's Oracle at Delphi, which spoke to Atalanta, was the most famous of Greek oracles.

ARCHER VS. BOAR

Atalanta and Meleager bring home the bacon.

Atalanta was known as a skilled archer and a very fast runner. Cast out of her home at birth by her father, who wanted a son, she was nursed by a bear and raised by hunters.

When Atalanta heard that King Oeneus of Calydon was organizing a hunt to catch an enormous wild boar that was terrorizing his kingdom, she decided to join the hunt.

Among the hunters were some of Greece's greatest heroes, including Jason, Heracles, and Theseus. But it was Atalanta who first wounded the boar. Then Meleager killed the beast. Meleager, who was in love with Atalanta, awarded her the boar's head and pelt, or fur. While this pleased Atalanta, who had a crush on Meleager, it got him into big trouble with his uncles, who thought they deserved the pelt.

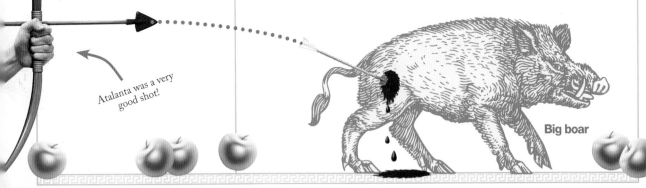

Atalanta was a very good shot!

Big boar

Atalanta

Melanion

easily distracted

clever!

ATALANTA'S RACE

A hopeful husband runs for his life.

On her return home from Calydon, Atalanta was told by the Oracle at Delphi that she should never marry. And when an oracle speaks, you'd better listen! But Atalanta's father, who had made amends with her, wanted her to get married. So she agreed— on one condition. She would challenge each man who wanted to marry her to a footrace. If the man won, Atalanta would marry him. But if she won, Atalanta would kill the challenger with a dart! Of course, Atalanta was confident that no one could beat her.

After Atalanta had raced (and killed) several men, Melanion made his move. Although he loved Atalanta with all his heart, he knew he couldn't outrun her. So he asked the goddess of love, Aphrodite, for help. She gave Melanion three golden apples and told him to drop them during the race. He did as he was told, and each time Atalanta paused to pick up an apple, Melanion surged ahead. To make a long race short, Melanion won the contest and Atalanta married him. They lived happily ever after … almost.

REALITY CHECK

According to J. Edgar Thompson, who named the city of Atlanta, Georgia, the name was chosen to honor former governor Wilson Lumpkin's daughter. Her middle name was Atalanta, after the fleet-footed goddess.

Want to know more? Go to:
http://ngeorgia.com/ang/Origin_of_the_name_Atlanta

CYBELE'S REVENGE

Atalanta and Melanion offend a goddess.

Atalanta and Melanion were very much in love. Maybe a little *too* much in love. When the goddess Cybele caught the pair cuddling in her temple, she blew a fuse! To punish the couple, she turned them into lions. Then, to add insult to injury, she yoked the pair of lions to her **chariot**.

In another version of the myth, it was on Zeus's sacred ground that the couple did their cuddling. Either way, the outcome was the same. Atalanta learned the hard way that the oracle is always right!

MYTHING LINK

Cybele was a goddess of nature and the earth. Long before the ancient Greeks worshipped her, she was worshipped by the Hittites and the Phrygians. The Greeks called her "Meter Oreie," meaning Mountain Mother. She was the patron goddess of caves, mountains, and wild animals, especially lions. No surprise there.

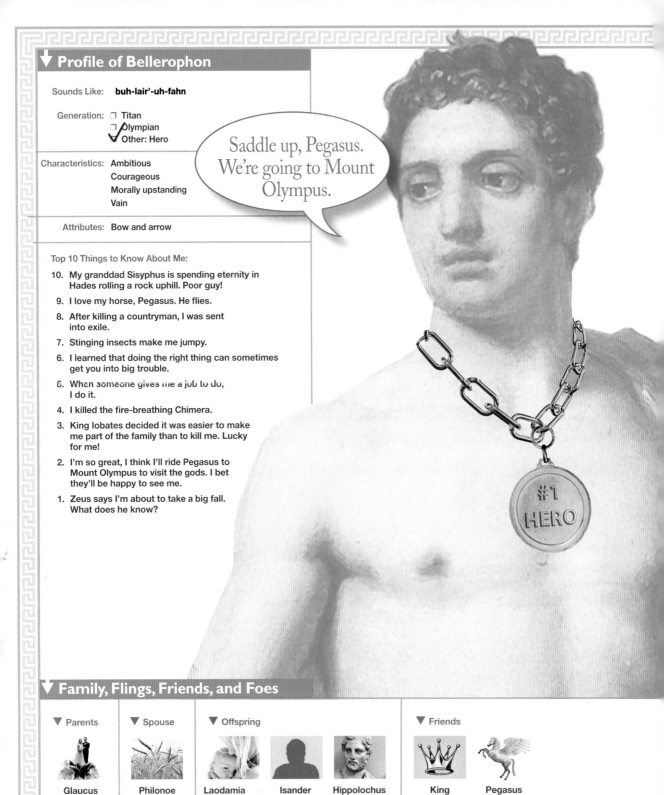

Profile of Bellerophon

Sounds Like: **buh-lair'-uh-fahn**

Generation: ☐ Titan
☐ Olympian
☑ Other: Hero

Characteristics: Ambitious
Courageous
Morally upstanding
Vain

Attributes: Bow and arrow

> Saddle up, Pegasus. We're going to Mount Olympus.

Top 10 Things to Know About Me:

10. My granddad Sisyphus is spending eternity in Hades rolling a rock uphill. Poor guy!

9. I love my horse, Pegasus. He flies.

8. After killing a countryman, I was sent into exile.

7. Stinging insects make me jumpy.

6. I learned that doing the right thing can sometimes get you into big trouble.

5. When someone gives me a job to do, I do it.

4. I killed the fire-breathing Chimera.

3. King Iobates decided it was easier to make me part of the family than to kill me. Lucky for me!

2. I'm so great, I think I'll ride Pegasus to Mount Olympus to visit the gods. I bet they'll be happy to see me.

1. Zeus says I'm about to take a big fall. What does he know?

#1 HERO

Family, Flings, Friends, and Foes

▼ Parents	▼ Spouse	▼ Offspring			▼ Friends	
Glaucus and Eurymede	Philonoe	Laodamia	Isander	Hippolochus	King Iobates	Pegasus

BELLEROPHON

FLYING HIGH

WHOOOO! Man, I am pumped! That Chimera is toast, baby! No little fire-breathing goat-lion-serpent monster is going to stand in my way. Amazons? Bring 'em on! No wonder Queen Stheneboea was crushin' on me. I have that effect on the ladies. But I'll let you in on a little secret. I'm tired of ordinary people and their ordinary problems. I was meant for *bigger* and *better* things. So look out, Mount Olympus, here I come!

REALITY CHECK

If you use your imagination, you can see the figure of Bellerophon's winged horse in the 18 stars that make up the constellation Pegasus.

Want to know more? Go to: http://www.kidsastronomy.com/astroskymap/constellation_hunt.htm

▼ Foes

King Proetus

Queen Stheneboea

The Chimera

Zeus

Pegasus

You sure you don't want to call first?

BELLEROPHON

"Giddyup."

MYTHLOPEDIA

Βελλεροφων

IT'S GREEK TO ME

Throughout history, monstrous creatures like the Chimera, with its fire-breathing abilities, have seemingly come to life in stories. The first mention of dragons in Western literature is in *The Iliad*. Author Homer describes a dragon design on Agamemnon's belt and breast plate. Such legendary heroes in English literature as St. George and Beowulf also fought and killed dragons, who symbolized the evil in the world.

Serpent tail

Goat head

Lion head and mane

A BEASTLY CHALLENGE

Bellerophon turns his back on a queen and faces a terrible monster.

While Bellerophon was visiting King Proetus of Argos, Proetus's wife, Queen Stheneboea, flirted with the handsome young man, but he rejected her advances. To get back at him, Stheneboea told her husband that their guest Bellerophon had been flirting with her. Angry that a guest would go after his wife, Proetus gave Bellerophon a note to take to Queen Stheneboea's father, King Iobates of Lycia. The note said: "Kill Bellerophon!" Bellerophon had been Iobates' guest for nine days

when the king finally got around to opening the note. Unwilling to kill a guest, the king devised a plan that he hoped would lead to Bellerophon's death: Bellerophon would have to kill the Chimera, a fire-breathing monster that was terrorizing the area. The king was certain the Chimera would scorch Bellerophon to a cinder.

Feeling sorry for Bellerophon, the goddess Athena gave him the magnificent winged horse Pegasus to ride. As the horse and rider approached the horrible monster, Bellerophon saw that it had the head and body of a lion, a goat's head protruding from its back, the tail of a serpent, and it breathed fire! The Chimera clawed and

Pegasus

Bellerophon

The Chimera

A pesky little menace from Zeus!

Pegasus

MOUNTAIN CLIMBING

A hero takes a ride and a tumble.

King Iobates was amazed that Bellerophon was able to kill the Chimera, so the king sent him on more dangerous quests, but Bellerophon successfully fulfilled every one. Iobates finally gave up trying to have Bellerophon killed and instead gave him his daughter's hand in marriage— along with half his kingdom.

All this success went to Bellerophon's head. In fact, he was so full of himself that he decided he belonged on Mount Olympus with the gods. So he hopped astride Pegasus and off they flew. Seeing the horse and rider approaching, Zeus, king of the gods, was outraged by

Bellerophon's arrogance. He had another idea. He sent a pesky fly to sting Pegasus, causing the horse to buck and throw Bellerophon back to Earth. Bellerophon landed hard. Badly injured and blinded by the fall, he spent the rest of his days wandering aimlessly, avoiding other people. A sad ending for a mighty hero.

shot flames at the pair, but Bellerophon and Pegasus swooped and swerved. Finally, with Pegasus hovering above the beast, Bellerophon took aim and killed it with his spear.

REALITY CHECK

The Chimera may have been real to Bellerophon, but today its name is used to describe a fanciful dream or imagining.

> "Giddyup, Pegasus, we're going to visit the gods."

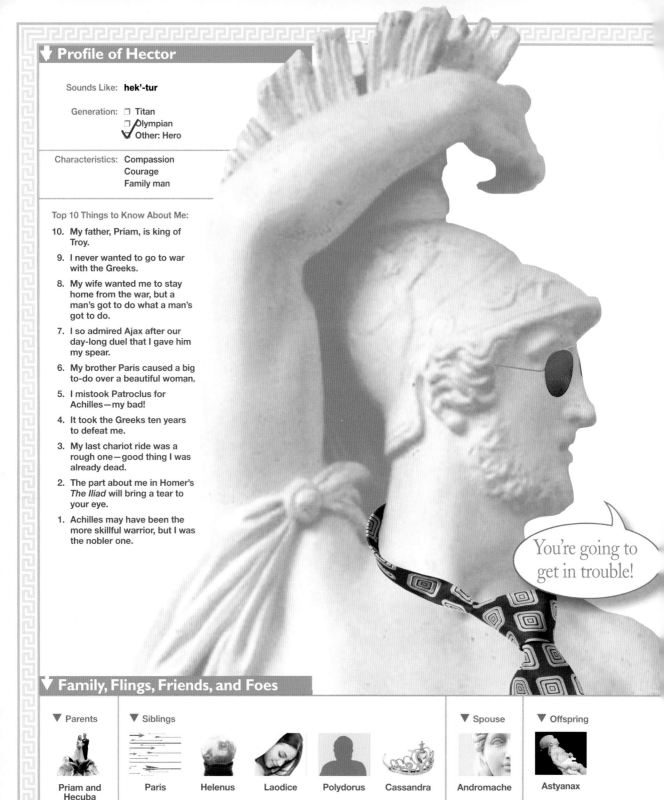

▼ Profile of Hector

Sounds Like: **hek'-tur**

Generation: ☐ Titan
☐ Olympian
☑ Other: Hero

Characteristics: Compassion
Courage
Family man

Top 10 Things to Know About Me:

10. My father, Priam, is king of Troy.

9. I never wanted to go to war with the Greeks.

8. My wife wanted me to stay home from the war, but a man's got to do what a man's got to do.

7. I so admired Ajax after our day-long duel that I gave him my spear.

6. My brother Paris caused a big to-do over a beautiful woman.

5. I mistook Patroclus for Achilles—my bad!

4. It took the Greeks ten years to defeat me.

3. My last chariot ride was a rough one—good thing I was already dead.

2. The part about me in Homer's *The Iliad* will bring a tear to your eye.

1. Achilles may have been the more skillful warrior, but I was the nobler one.

> You're going to get in trouble!

▼ Family, Flings, Friends, and Foes

▼ Parents	▼ Siblings					▼ Spouse	▼ Offspring
Priam and Hecuba	Paris	Helenus	Laodice	Polydorus	Cassandra	Andromache	Astyanax

HECTOR

BIG BROTHER

Paris, listen up: Helen is bad news. I'll admit that she's gorgeous; you've got great taste in women. But buddy, she's married! And her husband, Menelaus, is one tough dude. I wouldn't be surprised if he, like, started a war over her. There are other fish in the sea, bro. Plenty of girls are dying for the chance to date a prince from Troy—take it from me! So please, before it's too late, send Helen packing—or we'll all pay the price.

REALITY CHECK

The name Troy refers both to the remains of a Bronze Age fortress and city at Hissarlik in modern Turkey, near the entrance to the Dardanelles, and to the legendary city that was destroyed by ancient Greeks in the Trojan War.

Want to know more? Go to: http://www.mnsu.edu/emuseum/archaeology/sites/europe/hissarlik.html

> Sorry, bro. Are you talking to me?

Helen

Paris

▼ Friends

Ajax

▼ Foes

Paris

Helenus

Achilles

Patroclus

Εκτωρ

HECTOR

"And then a hero comes along …"

MYTH LOPEDIA

IT'S GREEK TO ME

Hector's tragic story and Achilles' triumphant one were told in Homer's epic poem *The Iliad*. In this touching passage from Samuel Butler's translation, Hector is about to head off to war, and he tries to comfort his son Astyanax:

"He stretched his arms towards his child, but the boy cried and nestled in his nurse's bosom, scared at the sight of his father's armour, and at the horse-hair plume that nodded fiercely from his helmet. Hector took the helmet from his head and laid it all gleaming upon the ground. Then he took his darling child, kissed him, and dandled him in his arms, praying over him the while to [Zeus] and to all the gods."

OFF TO WAR

A Greek warrior sulks and things look up for the Trojans.

Hector was the eldest son of King Priam of Troy. When his younger brother Paris kidnapped the beautiful Helen from Greece and took her home with him to Troy, Hector knew it was going to cause a problem. A big one.

He was soon proven right when Helen's kidnapping started the Trojan War.

Once the war began, Hector dedicated himself to the fight, becoming Troy's greatest warrior. But the Greek side was stacked with heroes. For nine years, the war raged on, with the Greeks having the upper hand. Then,

Trojan War

in the tenth year, the great warrior Achilles withdrew from the fight after he quarreled with Agamemnon about a captive woman.

Without Achilles, the Greeks began to lose. Not only that, at the request of Achilles' mother, Thetis, the mighty god Zeus had temporarily thrown his support behind the Trojans. Thetis and Zeus wanted to teach the Greeks a lesson about how to treat their star warrior. Meanwhile, Hector fought bravely and honorably for the Trojans.

While Achilles sulked in his tent and refused to fight, his best friend, Patroclus, borrowed his armor and horse-drawn **chariot** and joined the battle. Seeing the warrior's armor, Hector mistook Patroclus for Achilles and killed him. With his dying breath, Patroclus predicted that Hector's own death was near. Was Patroclus right? Read on!

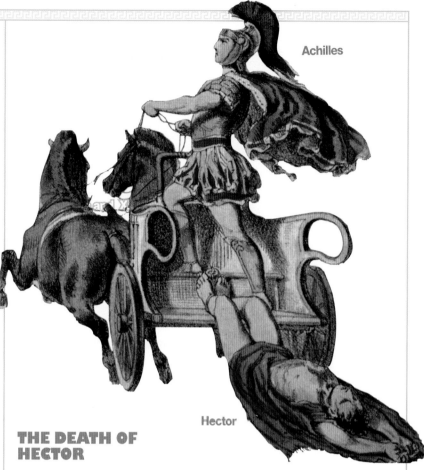

Achilles

Hector

THE DEATH OF HECTOR

Achilles challenges Hector to a showdown.

When Achilles heard that Hector had killed his beloved friend Patroclus, he was filled with grief and rage. He vowed revenge. The two warriors met for a final showdown. Achilles chased Hector around Troy three times, finally catching him. As Hector turned to attack, Achilles plunged his spear through a chink in the armor and pierced Hector's throat, killing the Trojan hero. Then Achilles tied Hector's dead body to the back of his chariot and dragged it around the walls of Troy.

At his mother's urging, Achilles returned Hector's body to his grieving father, King Priam. Hector was mourned for nine days, then his body was burned on a huge funeral **pyre**. Troy soon fell to the Greeks, but the noble warrior Hector's name lived on.

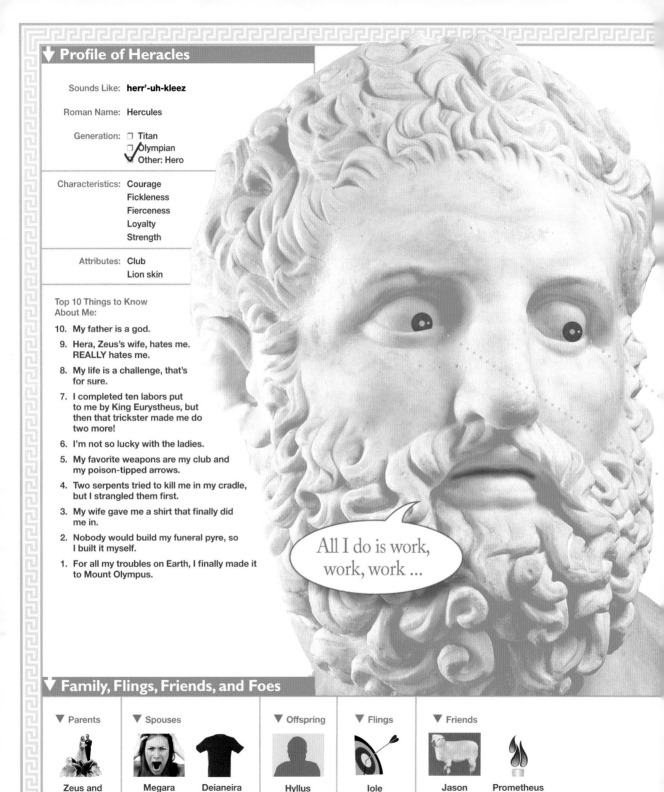

Profile of Heracles

Sounds Like:	**herr'-uh-kleez**
Roman Name:	**Hercules**
Generation:	☐ Titan ☑ Olympian ☑ Other: Hero

Characteristics: **Courage**
Fickleness
Fierceness
Loyalty
Strength

Attributes: **Club**
Lion skin

Top 10 Things to Know
About Me:

10. My father is a god.

9. Hera, Zeus's wife, hates me. REALLY hates me.

8. My life is a challenge, that's for sure.

7. I completed ten labors put to me by King Eurystheus, but then that trickster made me do two more!

6. I'm not so lucky with the ladies.

5. My favorite weapons are my club and my poison-tipped arrows.

4. Two serpents tried to kill me in my cradle, but I strangled them first.

3. My wife gave me a shirt that finally did me in.

2. Nobody would build my funeral pyre, so I built it myself.

1. For all my troubles on Earth, I finally made it to Mount Olympus.

All I do is work, work, work ...

Family, Flings, Friends, and Foes

▼ Parents	▼ Spouses		▼ Offspring	▼ Flings	▼ Friends	
Zeus and Alcmene	**Megara**	**Deianeira**	**Hyllus**	**Iole**	**Jason**	**Prometheus**

HERACLES

HERO FOR HIRE

What can I do for you? Are vicious monsters terrorizing your town? Ferocious beasts running wild? Is a vengeful goddess causing you grief? There's no monster too mean, no beast too big, and no labor too lowly—I'll tackle them all and be home in time for dinner! Limited time offer: Two-for-one Hero Special! That's right! Two impossible feats for one low price. I must be crazy to offer such a deal!

REALITY CHECK

The C-130 Hercules military aircraft takes its name from the mighty hero Hercules (Heracles), for whom no challenge was too great. It was originally designed to evacuate people in emergencies and transport cargo. Today it has many more uses, such as fighting fires and observing weather.

Want to know more? Go to: http://www.globalaircraft.org/planes/c-130_hercules.pl

> And take the garbage out!

▼ Foes

| Hera | Hydra | Nessus | King Eurystheus |

Hera

HERACLES

"I'm working for a livin'."

MYTHLOPEDIA

Ηρακλης

IT'S GREEK TO ME

There are a number of powerful groups in Greek mythology. The Titans were the children of Uranus and Gaea and were the first generation of gods. Led by Zeus, the Titans' children, known as the Olympians, defeated their parents in a battle called the Titanomachy.

Demigods were offspring born to a god and a human being, or **mortal**.

Heroes were extraordinary mortals who committed courageous deeds. Some heroes, such as Heracles, were granted immortality; others, such as Odysseus, remained mortal.

> "I chose to live a glorious life but it isn't easy."

SUPERBABY

Being the son of a god has its ups and downs.

The princess Alcmene was loved by the mighty god Zeus— along with about a gazillion other women! When she gave birth to Zeus's son Heracles, the baby had the strength of a demigod. Hera, Zeus's jealous wife, hated both Alcmene and her offspring, so she sent two serpents to kill the infant in his cradle. But Heracles was no ordinary baby. He strangled both serpents with his bare hands before they could lay a fang on him.

As a young man, Heracles had a vision. In the vision he was offered the choice of an easy life of pleasure or a more challenging life of hardship, danger, and glory. Heracles chose the second. And boy, did he ever get what he asked for!

REALITY CHECK

Under his Roman name, Hercules, Heracles has been the featured character in more than 70 movies and television films. Among the many actors who have portrayed him on the screen are Steve Reeves and Arnold Schwarzenegger. In 1997, Disney released *Hercules*, an animated version of Heracles' story.

Arnold Schwarzenegger

HERACLES AND MEGARA

Hera drives Heracles crazy.

Thebes, Heracles' hometown, was under attack from the armies of Orchomenus, a neighboring city. The young hero Heracles helped defend Thebes and defeat the enemy. Creon, the grateful king of Thebes, rewarded Heracles with his daughter Megara's hand in marriage. Heracles and Megara lived happily for a time and had several children. But the goddess Hera was still bent on destroying Heracles, so she drove him insane. While he was completely out of his mind, he killed Megara and their children. Once his sanity was restored, Heracles fled Thebes and visited the **Oracle** at Delphi, a priestess who spoke on behalf of the god Apollo. The oracle told him that to be cleansed of his terrible crime, he would have to serve King Eurystheus of Tiryns for twelve years.

REALITY CHECK

The legendary Thebes was actually a historic city. Once the most powerful city-state in ancient Greece, Thebes went to war against Athens in the Peloponnesian War in 431 BCE. Alexander the Great destroyed Thebes when it revolted against him in 316 BCE.

Want to know more? Go to:
http://www.sikyon.com/Thebes/thebes_eg.html

THE TWELVE LABORS OF HERACLES, 1–5

Eurystheus keeps Heracles busy. Really busy!

King Eurystheus and Heracles were cousins, but there was little family love between them. As the Oracle at Delphi had instructed, Heracles had to perform the following nearly impossible labors for the king:

1. Kill the ferocious Nemean Lion and make a cloak of its skin.

2. Kill the terrible Hydra of the Lernaean swamps. This enormous serpent had multiple heads. When one head was chopped off, Hydra immediately grew another. The task seemed impossible until Heracles had the bright idea to have his cousin Iolaus burn each stump after Heracles cut off one of Hydra's heads. This prevented the head from growing back, and soon Hydra was history.

3. Capture the golden-horned Cerynian stag.

4. Capture the Erymanthian boar.

5. Clean the Augean stables. King Augeas's stables held more cattle than any in Greece and had never

Hydra

been cleaned. Augeas told Heracles that if he could clean the stables in one day, he could have a tenth of the king's cattle. Heracles diverted the Rivers Alpheus and Peneus through the stables and the rushing waters washed out all the filth.

MYTHING LINK

Zeus's wife, Hera, didn't find it easy being married to the most powerful god on Mount Olympus. An Olympian and the goddess of women, marriage, and childbirth, she resisted Zeus's authority and was jealous of his other loves. But the most famous object of her hatred was Heracles. Hera tormented the hero from the day of his birth until the end of his mortal life.

THE TWELVE LABORS OF HERACLES, 6–12

A hero's work is never done.

After Heracles successfully completed his first five tasks, it was on to the next five (or so he thought!):

6. Chase away the man-eating, iron-feathered Stymphalian birds.

7. Capture the Cretan bull.

8. Capture the man-eating mares of Diomedes.

9. Retrieve the belt of Hippolyte, queen of the Amazons.

10. Round up the cattle of Geryon, a three-bodied giant.

With the ten labors completed, Heracles was ready for a rest. But Eurystheus was a sneaky character. He told Heracles that killing Hydra didn't count because Iolaus had helped him. And Eurystheus said cleaning the Augean stables didn't count either, because Heracles had cheated by using the rivers to wash away the dirt. So the king assigned poor Heracles two more tasks.

11. Collect the golden apples from the garden of the Hesperides.

12. Fetch Cerberus, the ferocious three-headed guard dog of the **Underworld**. For this task, Heracles entered the Underworld and asked its ruler, Hades, if he could take Cerberus to the upper world.

Hades agreed, but only if Heracles promised to **subdue** the vicious dog without using weapons. Heracles fought Cerberus until he lay helpless in the hero's powerful hands.

While Heracles was in the Underworld, he freed the hero Theseus, who had been trapped there; then he made his way to Earth. When Eurystheus saw Heracles approaching with Cerberus in his arms, he was so terrified that he leaped into a large jar called a *pithos* and begged Heracles to return the beast to the Underworld.

Finally, having completed all his chores, Heracles was rewarded by Eurystheus with his daughter Deianeira's hand in marriage.

REALITY CHECK

The Pillars of Heracles are two natural **promontories** that lie at the entrance of the Mediterranean Sea. One is in Spain and the other is on the north coast of Africa. According to legend, the two rocky landmarks were one until Heracles separated them with his great strength to make a path to Cadiz, Spain. For the ancient Greeks, the Pillars of Heracles marked the boundary of the known world.

Want to know more? Go to: http://phoenicia.org/ gibraltar.html

Gotcha!

Heracles

Cretan bull

Heracles

That shirt is hot!

THE KILLER SHIRT

A wily Centaur gets revenge from beyond the grave.

Heracles and Deianeira were a happily married couple. But tragedy continued to stalk the hero. One day Deianeira and Heracles came to a river. Heracles swam across it, but Deianeira hesitated. Nessus, a wicked **Centaur**, offered to carry her across to the other side. She agreed, but the Centaur attempted to kidnap her while Heracles was busy swimming. Heracles saw the Centaur's trick and shot him with an arrow that had been dipped in the poisonous blood of the monstrous Hydra. As Nessus lay dying, he plotted his vengeance. He gave Deianeira his shirt, stained with Hydra's blood, claiming it had magical properties. He told her that if

she ever felt in danger of losing Heracles' love, she should ask Heracles to put on the shirt and he would never leave her.

Years later, Heracles fell in love with the princess Iole. Fearing she would lose her husband, Deianeira followed Nessus's advice and gave the Centaur's shirt to Heracles as a gift. When Heracles put on the shirt, the poisonous blood of Hydra seeped into his skin and made him burn in torment. Unable to remove the terrible shirt, Heracles pulled several trees from the earth and built himself a funeral **pyre**, then set it on fire. As he lay on the pyre, his **immortal** part returned to Mount Olympus, where he and Hera finally made peace. Then the hero rose to the heavens as the constellation Heracles.

MYTHING LINK

Centaurs in Greek mythology were half-horse and half-man creatures. They were known for being aggressive and mischievous. But not all Centaurs were as bad as Nessus, the wicked Centaur whose shirt killed Heracles. Chiron, the most famous Centaur, was a wise teacher whose students included such great heroes as Achilles, Heracles, and Jason.

Chiron

HERACLES' TO-DO LIST

Twelve challenging chores ...
four down, eight to go.

Slay the Nemean Lion

Capture the Erymanthian boar

Capture the Cretan bull

Bring back the cattle of Geryon

Slay the many-headed Hydra

Capture the Cerynian stag

Clean the Augean stables in a day

Chase away the Stymphalian birds

Steal the mares of Diomedes

Bring back the belt of Hippolyte

Collect the apples of the Hesperides

Capture Cerberus

Sounds Like: **jay'-suhn**

Generation: ☐ Titan
☐ Olympian
☑ Other: Hero

Characteristics: Bravery
Resourcefulness
Treacherousness
Unfaithfulness

Attributes: The *Argo*
Golden Fleece

Top 10 Things to Know About Me:

10. My wife, Medea, is a real witch.

9. My uncle Pelias stole my throne out from under me.

8. I think the Argonauts are a great bunch of guys to go on a quest with.

7. I haven't met a king yet that I can trust— and that includes me.

6. I love my ship, the *Argo*, my home away from home.

5. I never want to see another fire-breathing ox.

4. I wouldn't have planted those dragon's teeth if I had known they would come back to bite me!

3. Like I always say, let sleepless dragons lie.

2. The gods didn't like the way I treated Medea. Too bad!

1. After all this time, I *still* don't know what to do with a Golden Fleece.

> I'm coming for you, little lamb!

▼ Family, Flings, Friends, and Foes

▼ Parents	▼ Spouse	▼ Offspring		▼ Flings	▼ Friends		
Aeson and Alcimede	Medea	Thessalus	Alcimenes	Creusa	Castor and Pollux	Heracles	Peleus

JASON

FLEECED

Stay back! I'm warning you—I'm trained in self-defense! Suspicious? Me? You'd be suspicious, too, if people had been after you for your whole life! First, my uncle tried to kill me on a wild Golden Fleece chase. Next, Aietes sent fire-breathing oxen after me— and you don't even want to know what he did after that! Then I married Medea, a total witch. She murdered my girlfriend and my sons to get even with me! You know, it's not paranoia if people are actually out to get you!

Golden Fleece

▼ Foes

Pelias

Aietes

Medea

Baaad man!

JASON

"I'm counting sheep!"

MYTH LOPEDIA

Ιασων

IT'S GREEK TO ME

The 50 **Argonauts** who accompanied Jason on his quest for the **Golden Fleece** included some of the bravest and strongest heroes and heroines of Greek mythology. Among the notables were:

Atalanta	Orpheus
Meleager	Peleus
Castor and Pollux	Telamon
Heracles	

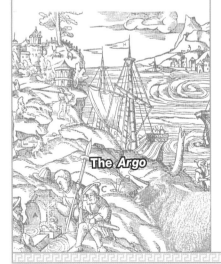

The *Argo*

THE QUEST FOR THE GOLDEN FLEECE

Jason finds the fleece—but It's not an easy job.

Jason was the son of King Aeson and Queen Alcimede of Iolcus. In a struggle for power, Jason's uncle Pelias seized the throne of King Aeson. Then Pelias killed most of Aeson's heirs. Alcimede escaped with Jason and left him in the care of the wise Centaur Chiron.

When he was 20, Jason returned to Iolcus to take back the kingdom that was rightfully his. Pelias promised to make Jason king, but not until Jason acquired the fabled Golden Fleece of Colchis. Jason agreed to the deal, not realizing that Pelias was counting on his nephew to never return from the dangerous quest.

With the help of the goddess Athena, master builder Epeius made Jason a magical ship, the *Argo*, for his quest. The sailors who joined Jason on the quest were known as the Argonauts. On their mission, Jason and the Argonauts overcame stormy seas, terrifying monsters, and the seductive song of the Sirens, island-dwelling women who lured many sailors to shipwreck.

When Jason and the crew arrived at Colchis, King Aietes agreed to give them the Golden Fleece if Jason first completed three tasks. Aietes' daughter Medea, a **sorceress**, had fallen in love with Jason and promised to help him with the tasks.

First, Jason had to yoke together two fire-breathing oxen

Jason

fleece

dragon

and plow a field. Medea gave Jason a special ointment to put on that prevented him from being burned by the oxen's fiery breath while he plowed. With that, he successfully completed the first task.

Next, Jason had to plant dragons' teeth in the soil he had plowed. When the teeth were planted, an army of soldiers sprang up and attacked Jason and his crew. Jason grabbed a boulder and tossed it at the soldiers. Confused, the soldiers began fighting each other until they were all dead.

Finally, Jason had to get past the sleepless dragon that guarded the Golden Fleece. Medea gave Jason a magic potion that put the dragon to sleep. Jason seized the fleece, and he, Medea, and the Argonauts safely returned to the *Argo*.

JASON AND MEDEA

Jason betrays Medea and pays with his life.

When the *Argo* returned to Iolcus, Jason presented the Golden Fleece to Pelias. Medea, now married to Jason, knew that Pelias would never give up the throne to his nephew. So she convinced Pelias's daughters that they could restore their father's youth by cutting him up and cooking the pieces.

With Pelias out of the way, Jason seized power. But he was defeated in battle by Pelias's son Acastus, who took over the throne and **exiled** Jason.

Jason and Medea sought **refuge** in Corinth. There, Jason fell in love with Creusa, daughter of King Creon. Jason planned to divorce Medea and marry Creusa, believing he could one day take over Creon's kingdom.

Betrayed, Medea vowed vengeance. She sent Creusa a dress as a wedding gift. When the unsuspecting bride put it on, it stuck to her skin and burned her and her father to death. Medea wasn't done. To further

Let our fleeces go!

punish Jason, she killed their two sons. Then she escaped in a **chariot** provided by her grandfather Helios, the sun god, and fled to Athens. Jason returned to Iolcus, where he defeated Acastus and retook the throne. His betrayal of Medea, however, put him out of favor with the gods. Condemned to wander aimlessly, Jason arrived in Corinth, where he lay down to sleep in the shadow of the rotting *Argo*. The ship collapsed on him and killed him, ending the life of one of the greatest—and sneakiest—Greek heroes.

REALITY CHECK

According to legend, Jason founded the city now known as Ljubljana, capital of the Eastern European nation of Slovenia. The story says the *Argo* sailed up the Danube River and into the Baltic Sea to the site of Ljubljana, originally called Aemona. The city's coat of arms bears a dragon, a symbol of Jason and his adventures.

Want to know more? Go to: http://www.visitljubljana.si/

Ljubljana

▼ Profile of Meleager

Sounds Like: mel-ee-ay'-jur

Generation: ☐ Titan
☐ Olympian
☑ Other: Hero

Special Abilities: Hunting

Characteristics: Bravery
Generosity
Rashness

Top 10 Things to Know About Me:

10. I sailed with Jason and the Argonauts.

9. My dad was king of Calydon.

8. I have a thing for strong women.

7. Boars are my business.

6. My hunting buddies were Jason, Theseus, Heracles, and Atalanta.

5. I'm no hog when it comes to sharing the glory.

4. My uncles couldn't be more "boarish."

3. I always say that there's more than one way to skin a pig.

2. I was done in by an angry mom and a burning log.

1. Now I believe in the Fates for sure!

Is something burning?

▼ Family, Flings, Friends, and Foes

▼ Parents	▼ Uncles		▼ Flings	▼ Friends			▼ Foes
Oeneus and Althaea	Toxeus	Plexippus	Atalanta	Heracles	Jason	Theseus	Atalanta

MELEAGER

BURN, BABY, BURN

Mom, you look pretty today! Is that a new tunic? It really brings out the color of your eyes! Is it warm in here, or is it just me? Oh, you're cold? Let me add more wood to the fire. No, let *me*. I'll just run out and chop down a tree. We wouldn't want to burn the wrong log, remember? The one the Fates said would end my life when it finished burning? What? No, I'm not nervous. There's no reason for me to be nervous, right? *Right, Mom?*

REALITY CHECK

Boar hunting was a popular sport in ancient Greece. Today, boars live in Central Europe, Northern Africa, and many parts of Asia. They live in groups called sounders and eat everything from grass and berries to insects and small mammals.

Want to know more? Go to: http://www.sandiegozoo.org/ animalbytes/t-wild_swine.html

Althaea

The Fates

Μελεαγρος

MELEAGER

"Feeling hot, hot, hot!"

MYTHLOPEDIA

IT'S GREEK TO ME

In Greek mythology, the Fates were three goddesses who would arrive just after a baby's birth to determine its destiny, or life span. They are usually represented as three old women who control the thread of life. Clotho spins the thread, Lachesis measures it out, and Atropos cuts it.

The Fates

MELEAGER'S FATE

Althaea saves her baby boy.

When Meleager was born, the Fates told his mother, Althaea, that her son would live only as long as a certain log in her hearth continued to burn. Once the log had turned to ash, Meleager would die. Wanting to protect her baby, the worried mom thought quickly, then snatched the log from the flames and hid it in a chest.

Meleager grew up to become a mighty warrior. He was among the **Argonauts** who accompanied the hero Jason on his quest for the **Golden Fleece**. His mother's quick action had spared the hero—for a while, anyway.

That is no ordinary log!

DO NOT BURN

THE CALYDONIAN BOAR HUNT

Atalanta strikes first, but Meleager wins the hunt.

At one time, Meleager's father, King Oeneus, had failed to make a sacrifice to Artemis, the goddess of the hunt. Furious at this offense, Artemis sent an enormous wild boar to terrorize the kingdom.

Oeneus ordered Meleager to gather all the great heroes in a hunt for the Calydonian boar. Among those who joined the hunt were: Jason, of Golden Fleece fame; Theseus, slayer of the Minotaur (a vicious human-eating half bull, half man that lived in a **labyrinth**); the mighty hero Heracles; and the fleet-footed Atalanta, also a great hunter. Of all the skilled hunters, it was Atalanta who first wounded the boar. Then Meleager killed the beast. In love with Atalanta, Meleager awarded her the boar's pelt, or fur.

UP IN SMOKE

In a fit of anger, Althaea throws another log on the fire.

Meleager's gift of the Calydonian boar's pelt melted Atalanta's heart but it angered his uncles Toxeus and Plexippus, who thought they deserved the precious pelt. The three men began to argue; then they got into a violent struggle, during which Meleager killed both his uncles.

When Meleager's mother, Althaea, heard the news about her brothers, she was furious with her son. She opened the chest in which she had hidden the ill-fated log and tossed it into the fire. As the flames turned the log to ash, Meleager withered away and finally died. Then, full of remorse, Althaea killed herself.

"Hey, Mom! Where are you taking that log?"

Atalanta

Meleager

Boar

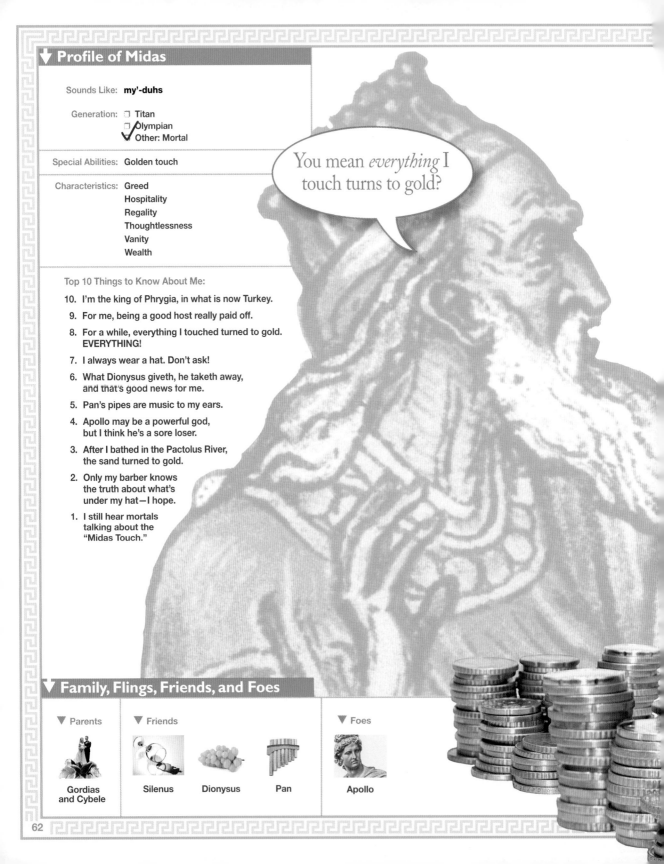

▼ Profile of Midas

Sounds Like: **my'-duhs**

Generation: ☐ Titan
☐ Olympian
☑ Other: Mortal

Special Abilities: Golden touch

Characteristics: Greed
Hospitality
Regality
Thoughtlessness
Vanity
Wealth

> You mean *everything* I touch turns to gold?

Top 10 Things to Know About Me:

10. I'm the king of Phrygia, in what is now Turkey.

9. For me, being a good host really paid off.

8. For a while, everything I touched turned to gold. EVERYTHING!

7. I always wear a hat. Don't ask!

6. What Dionysus giveth, he taketh away, and that's good news for me.

5. Pan's pipes are music to my ears.

4. Apollo may be a powerful god, but I think he's a sore loser.

3. After I bathed in the Pactolus River, the sand turned to gold.

2. Only my barber knows the truth about what's under my hat—I hope.

1. I still hear mortals talking about the "Midas Touch."

▼ Family, Flings, Friends, and Foes

▼ Parents	▼ Friends			▼ Foes
Gordias and Cybele	Silenus	Dionysus	Pan	Apollo

MIDAS
GOLDFINGER

Aw, snap! Check this out, player—anything I touch turns to gold! Dionysus knows that I'm the host with the most. That's why he gave me the magic touch. One tap of my finger and bam! I'm bringing the bling, baby! You like my gold shoes? My gold oak tree? My gold bed? Oh, bam! Can you help me out, friend? My nose itches. To tell you the truth, turning everything to gold is not as great as it seems— I'm getting a little hungry!

REALITY CHECK

In the eighth century BCE, a real King Midas ruled in Phrygia, in what is now Turkey. His tomb was discovered in 1959. The legend of Midas's golden touch may have arisen from a Greek misconception that Phrygia was a land of great wealth.

Want to see some Phrygian art? Go to: http://www.metmuseum.org/ toah/hd/phry/hd_phry.htm

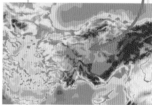

MIDAS

"I've got the magic touch."

MYTHLOPEDIA

Μιδας

IT'S GREEK TO ME

Satyrs were rowdy woodland creatures in Greek mythology They were a mixture of man and animal. Their upper bodies were human and their lower bodies, legs, and hooves resembled those of a horse (in later stories, a goat). They also had little horns, pointed ears, and tails. Satyrs enjoyed frolicking with their female counterparts, nature spirits called **nymphs**.

Satyr

MIDAS'S GOLDEN WISH

His wish comes true but it's more than Midas can handle.

Silenus was the oldest of the satyrs. He was the teacher of Dionysus, the god of fertility and wine making. One day, Silenus had wandered off and become lost in Phrygia. Some local people found him and took him to the court of Midas, their king. A charming host, Midas welcomed his unexpected guest and let him stay in his palace for ten days. Then he brought Silenus back to Dionysus. The god was so grateful to Midas for this act of kindness that he promised to grant the king whatever he wished for. So Midas wished that everything he touched would turn to gold.

For hours Midas delighted in turning everything within reach to gold—stones, chairs, pots, and more. When dinnertime arrived, the king sat down at his banquet table to eat. But each morsel of food he touched turned to gold before he could take a bite. So did his cup of wine. Midas grew more hungry—and worried—as he realized that his gift would cause him to starve or die of thirst!

Midas rushed to Dionysus and pleaded with him to take back his gift. Dionysus explained that to get rid of his unwanted power, the king would have to bathe in the Pactolus River. After Midas's dip in the river, its sands were filled with gold!

He's happy now, but just wait!

Midas

Apollo

Pan

Judge

Midas

GRECIAN IDOL

Midas messes with the wrong musician!

When Midas no longer had the gift of the golden touch, he wanted a simpler life, so he moved from his palace to a place in the country. There he became friends with Pan, the god of nature, who entertained him by playing tunes on his pipes.

One day Pan challenged Apollo, the god of **prophecy** and music, to a musical contest. Midas agreed to be a judge. Apollo dazzled the judges, plucking and strumming his **lyre**. Then Pan blew a pretty tune on his pipes. When the judges cast their votes, all but one picked Apollo: Midas voted for Pan.

What an insult for the god of music! To show his displeasure, Apollo gave Midas a gift—the long, floppy ears of a donkey.

Midas was so embarrassed by his donkey ears that he kept them hidden under a hat. The only person to ever see them was his barber, who was sworn to secrecy. But the barber had to tell somebody, so he dug a hole in the ground and whispered the secret into it. Reeds grew out of the soil that filled the hole and when the wind blew, the reeds could be heard to whisper, "King Midas has donkey ears."

MYTHING LINK

Pan was the Greek god of nature. He looked much like a satyr—half man and half goat.

REALITY CHECK

The legend of Midas's golden touch may have been a way to explain the gold extracted for many years from the real Pactolus River that runs near the Aegean Sea in Turkey. The gold enriched the economy of the ancient land of Lydia, where Dionysus supposedly lived.

Donkey ears

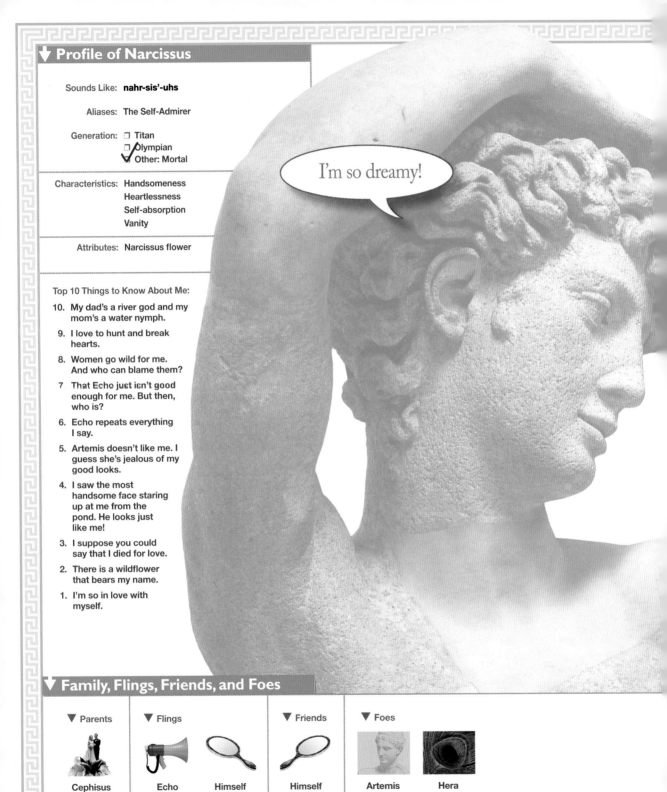

▼ Profile of Narcissus

Sounds Like: nahr-sis'-uhs

Aliases: The Self-Admirer

Generation: ☐ Titan
☐ Olympian
☑ Other: Mortal

Characteristics: Handsomeness
Heartlessness
Self-absorption
Vanity

Attributes: Narcissus flower

I'm so dreamy!

Top 10 Things to Know About Me:

10. My dad's a river god and my mom's a water nymph.

9. I love to hunt and break hearts.

8. Women go wild for me. And who can blame them?

7. That Echo just isn't good enough for me. But then, who is?

6. Echo repeats everything I say.

5. Artemis doesn't like me. I guess she's jealous of my good looks.

4. I saw the most handsome face staring up at me from the pond. He looks just like me!

3. I suppose you could say that I died for love.

2. There is a wildflower that bears my name.

1. I'm so in love with myself.

▼ Family, Flings, Friends, and Foes

▼ Parents	▼ Flings		▼ Friends	▼ Foes	
Cephisus and Leirope	Echo	Himself	Himself	Artemis	Hera

NARCISSUS

HELLO, HANDSOME!

Aren't I a sight for sore eyes! I've never seen anyone so good-looking. Who could guess that a creature as handsome as me would live in this pond? Wait, I can't see myself with all the ripples on the water—does anybody have a mirror? (I have to stop kissing my reflection!) Oh, thank gods, there I am. Just look at me. Is that a face? Look at those dimples. Those eyes. *Sigh.* I could just gaze at myself for the rest of my life!

Back atcha!

REALITY CHECK

The narcissus flower generally blooms in the spring. A member of the amaryllis family, it is often known by its common English name, daffodil.

Ναρκισσος

NARCISSUS

MYTH LOPEDIA

IT'S GREEK TO ME

In Greek mythology, **nymphs** are beautiful young women who are among the lesser goddesses. They are often associated with a particular place, object, or force in nature, such as water, mountains, or woodlands. Many are gentle and loving, but some are wild and vengeful. Famous nymphs include: Thetis, the mother of Achilles; Calypso, who loved the hero Odysseus; Daphne, who was loved by the god Apollo; Metis, the first wife of Zeus; and Syrinx, who was **transformed** into hollow reeds by the god Pan.

"If you looked this good, I'd love you, too!"

HERA'S REVENGE

Echo's gift of gab gets her in trouble.

Narcissus was a handsome youth who loved only himself. All the nymphs thought he was gorgeous and tried to get his attention, but Narcissus was completely full of himself and ignored them. The nymph who loved him the most was Echo. In fact, the only thing Echo loved more than Narcissus was the sound of her own voice.

"Echo can really talk your ear off!"

The mighty god Zeus put Echo's talent for talking to his own use. Whenever the god was visiting another nymph—and that happened often—Echo would distract Zeus's wife, Hera, with her **incessant** chatter. When Hera found out why Echo was always talking her ear off, she put a curse on the nymph. From then on, Echo could only repeat the words that another person said to her.

Hmmm! I know that guy!

Narcissus

68

NO ANSWER FOR NARCISSUS

Echo fades away … fades away … fades away.

The nymph Echo was an attendant of Artemis, the goddess of the hunt. One day the chatty nymph followed Narcissus when he was hunting in the forest. When Narcissus saw her lurking behind a tree, he called out, "Who are you?" All poor Echo could say in reply was: "Who are you?" This went on for some time. Finally in desperation, Echo threw herself at Narcissus's feet, but he just stepped over her and continued walking.

Feeling sad and rejected, Echo went off by herself into the mountains. She gradually wasted away from her broken heart. All that remained was her voice— the echo.

ARTEMIS'S SPELL

Narcissus falls in love with the best-looking guy around.

The goddess Artemis vowed revenge on Narcissus for his cold-hearted treatment of Echo. She put a spell on the self-centered youth as he walked through the woods. When Narcissus stopped at a pond to get a drink, he saw his reflection in the water and thought it was another person—and a good-looking one, at that!

As Narcissus took a drink, the water rippled and the image disappeared. Narcissus waited patiently until the reflection reappeared in the water. When it did, Narcissus tried to embrace it, but the image didn't move. Narcissus was so captivated by his own reflection that he neither drank nor ate, and he gradually wasted away. Artemis took pity

Narcissus

on the youth and transformed him into the wildflower that bears his name, the narcissus.

REALITY CHECK

Narcissus's preoccupation with himself lives on in the psychological condition called narcissism. Narcissists are so obsessed with themselves that they are unable to have emotional relationships with other people.

Want to know more? Go to:
http://www.mayoclinic.com/health/narcissistic-personality-disorder/DS00652

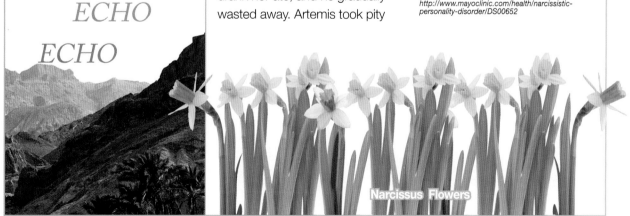

Narcissus Flowers

▼ Profile of Odysseus

Sounds Like: oh-dis'-ee-uhs

Roman Name: Ulysses (or Ulixes)

Aliases: No Man

Generation:
- ☐ Titan
- ☐ Olympian
- ☑ Other: Hero

Characteristics:
Cleverness
Courage
Daring
Eloquence
Persistence
Resourcefulness
Ruthlessness
Wisdom

Top 10 Things to Know About Me:

10. I'm about as clever as they come.

9. I was the brains behind the Trojan Horse, even though Athena gets all the credit.

8. Poseidon made sure my journey home was a rough one.

7. I used a sharp stick to fix a dumb Cyclops but good.

6. I'm the main character of Homer's *The Odyssey*.

5. I can be easily distracted from a goal—especially by a beautiful woman.

4. One thing I'd advise you: Don't eat the meat on Thrinacia.

3. I left home a king and came back a beggar.

2. I didn't really want to kill Penelope's suitors, but they just got in my face.

1. Next time somebody starts a war in a faraway place, I'm staying home.

▼ Family, Flings, Friends, and Foes

▼ Parents	▼ Spouse	▼ Offspring	▼ Flings		▼ Friends		
Laertes and Anticleia	Penelope	Telemachus	Calypso	Circe	Achilles	Menelaus	Athena

ODYSSEUS

LOST

Truth time: I have no idea where we are. Don't tell the crew, okay? Not that they'd care. Ever since we landed on that island and they ate "crazy fruit," they've forgotten everything. Seriously, the islands have been nothing but trouble. I'll never forget being trapped on that creepy island with those one-eyed weirdos. We're lucky any of us got out alive! And now my crew is pigging out at that strange Circe's house. At this rate, we'll never get home!

REALITY CHECK

With no instruments to guide them, ancient sailors relied on celestial navigation to chart their course at sea. Celestial navigation uses the position of the stars and planets to determine direction at sea. For example, by finding the North Star and measuring its distance from the horizon, sailors can figure out their latitude, or distance from the equator.

Want to know more? Go to: http://www.astronomy.com/asy/default.aspx?c=a&id=2287

▼ Foes

Polyphemus   Poseidon   The Trojans   The Cyclopes   Helios

ODYSSEUS

"Does anybody have a map?"

MYTHLOPEDIA

Οδυσσευς

IT'S GREEK TO ME

Homer is the legendary Greek poet who is said to have written *The Odyssey*, but that may not be completely accurate. For one thing, *written* is probably the wrong word, because ancient poets told their stories orally. Today, many experts believe this great **epic** poem was handed down from storyteller to storyteller over many generations. So, it is likely that Homer was not the sole author of *The Odyssey*.

> "I never thought getting home would be harder than fighting a war."

ODYSSEUS AND THE TROJAN WAR

A great hero dreams up a big surprise.

Odysseus was the son of King Laertes of Ithaca. When the Trojan War began, an **oracle** told Odysseus that if he went to Troy it would be many years before he returned home. That was enough to convince him to find a way not to leave. Clever Odysseus made believe he was a fool. When the Greek leaders came to get him, they found him plowing his fields with a collection of different animals yoked to the plow. He ignored them completely, until one equally clever Greek placed Odysseus's infant child right in the path of his plow. When Odysseus stopped plowing because he was afraid of hurting the child, the Greeks knew he wasn't crazy!

So Odysseus went to Troy after all and became one of the Greeks' most important leaders. It was Odysseus who persuaded Achilles, the greatest of Greek warriors, to join the Greeks at Troy. When Achilles was killed in battle, Odysseus persuaded Achilles' son Pyrrhus to take his father's place in the war.

Trojan Horse

Odysseus's greatest contribution to the Greek victory at Troy was the Trojan Horse. His plan was to offer an enormous wooden horse to the Trojans, supposedly as a gift to the goddess Athena. The horse was built by Epeius, builder of the *Argo*, the magical ship that carried Jason and the **Argonauts** in their quest for the **Golden Fleece**. A group of Greek warriors hid inside the horse, while the remaining Greeks pretended to sail for home. The unsuspecting Trojans accepted the gift horse and wheeled it into their city. They set it before the temple of Athena and then went off to celebrate the end of the fighting. During the night, the Greeks, led by Odysseus, unlocked the gates to the city and the Greek army poured in. Soon Troy fell, and it was the Greeks who celebrated. And all thanks to that crafty Odysseus!

THE JOURNEY HOME

Odysseus's crew stops in the land of the Lotus Eaters and forgets where they're going.

Although the Greeks won the Trojan War, they were not out of danger. The goddess Athena was angry with them for the hero Agamemnon's rough treatment of the Trojan princess Cassandra, whom he had captured and enslaved. Poseidon vowed that none of the Greeks would have an easy time returning home, especially Odysseus.

On the journey, the ship carrying Odysseus and his men was **buffeted** by stormy seas.

When they finally came ashore on an island, Odysseus sent out a small group to explore the area. The explorers came upon a group of locals who generously offered their guests the fruit of the lotus. This fruit caused those who ate it to forget their homeland and made them want to stay on the island in a dreamy trance. But Odysseus, who hadn't eaten the fruit, dragged his men back to their ship to continue the voyage home to Ithaca.

REALITY CHECK

The story of Odysseus's wanderings on his way home from the Trojan War is the central theme of Homer's epic *The Odyssey*. Because of its strong narrative and dramatic action, this poem has been called the "first novel" by many critics.

Want to know more? Go to:
http://www.mythweb.com/odyssey/

Do NOT eat this or you will be on permanent vacation!

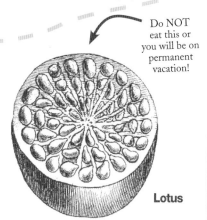

Lotus

ODYSSEUS AND THE CYCLOPES

A hero tricks a hungry Cyclops.

Continuing their journey home, Odysseus and his crew landed on an island. Searching for food and shelter, the men entered a cave. Little did they suspect that the cozy cavern was the home of the Cyclops Polyphemus, a huge shepherd who happened to be a son of the sea god Poseidon. In fact, the entire island was inhabited by one-eyed, man-eating Cyclopes!

That evening, when Polyphemus returned to the cave with his flock of sheep and found a bunch of sailors eating his food and making themselves at home, he rolled a boulder across the entrance, trapping the men

inside. Then he set about making a feast of the crew. That night, he ate two men for dinner. The next morning, he ate two more for breakfast. And guess what the Cyclops had for lunch? Two more men!

With time and men running out, Odysseus came up with a plan. He offered Polyphemus some wine and struck up a conversation. When the Cyclops asked his name, Odysseus answered, "No Man." As Odysseus continued to talk, Polyphemus fell sound asleep.

While the monster snored, Odysseus and his remaining men sharpened an olive branch

into a spear and stuck it into the giant's one eye. Polyphemus screamed, and the other Cyclopes on the island came running to the entrance of the cave. When they asked Polyphemus who was hurting him, he replied, "No Man!" "What?" they shouted. "No Man is hurting me," answered Polyphemus. Certain that Polyphemus was losing his mind, the other Cyclopes went away.

The next morning, when Polyphemus let his sheep out of the cave, Odysseus and his men held onto the undersides of the sheep and escaped to their ship. Polyphemus angrily hurled boulders at the ship, but missed because he couldn't see. The frustrated Cyclops begged his father, Poseidon, to prevent Odysseus from getting home to Ithaca, or at least to make sure that Odysseus's men died first. That way, the hero would have to get home aboard a stranger's ship. Poseidon vowed to fulfill part of his son's wish.

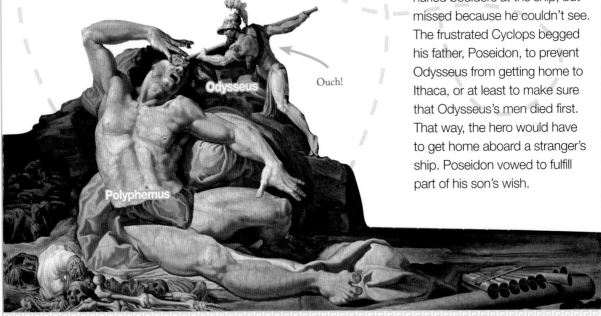

Odysseus

Ouch!

Polyphemus

ARE WE THERE YET?

Odysseus takes the long way home.

After their run-in with the Cyclopes, was it smooth sailing for Odysseus and his crew? No such luck.

- On Aeaea, the **sorceress** Circe turned Odysseus's men into pigs! Immune to her magic but not to her charms, Odysseus fell in love with Circe and stayed for a year.
- To get past the Sirens, a group of sea **nymphs** whose haunting songs lured sailors to their death, the crew plugged their ears with beeswax and Odysseus lashed himself to the mast.
- At Thrinacia, Odysseus's men had a cookout—with beef from Helios's herd of sacred cattle. Enraged, Helios asked Zeus for help. So the mighty god struck the ship with a thunderbolt, wrecking the boat and killing everyone but Odysseus.
- Rescued by the Phaeacians, Odysseus boarded one of their ships and headed home to Ithaca. But his problems weren't over yet!

HOME AT LAST

Odysseus surprises his wife and kills the competition.

Odysseus (in disguise)

For the ten years that her husband, Odysseus, had been trying to get home from the war, Penelope didn't know if he was alive or dead. In the meantime, other men had their eyes on the empty throne of the missing king.

They crowded around Penelope, urging her to give up on her long-lost hubby. Penelope did her best to fend them off, but they hung around the palace, ate her food, drank her wine, and generally made pests of themselves.

Odysseus finally reached Ithaca. With the help of the goddess Athena, who had come to like this crafty fellow, Odysseus shrewdly disguised himself as a beggar. Penelope did not recognize the beggar when he entered the great hall. She announced to all the men who had gathered there that her next husband would be the man who could string Odysseus's bow and shoot an arrow through twelve axe-handles. None of them was strong enough to string the bow. Then the beggar stepped forward, strung the bow, and shot an arrow through all twelve handles. As the other men looked on in amazement, Odysseus threw off his disguise. With the help of his son, Telemachus, Odysseus killed all the men. Home, at last.

Helios

PROPERTY OF HELIOS

Helios's cows

WHERE'S ODYSSEUS?

A hero and his crew take the long way home. See if you can follow Odysseus as he makes his way from Ithaca to Troy and back again.

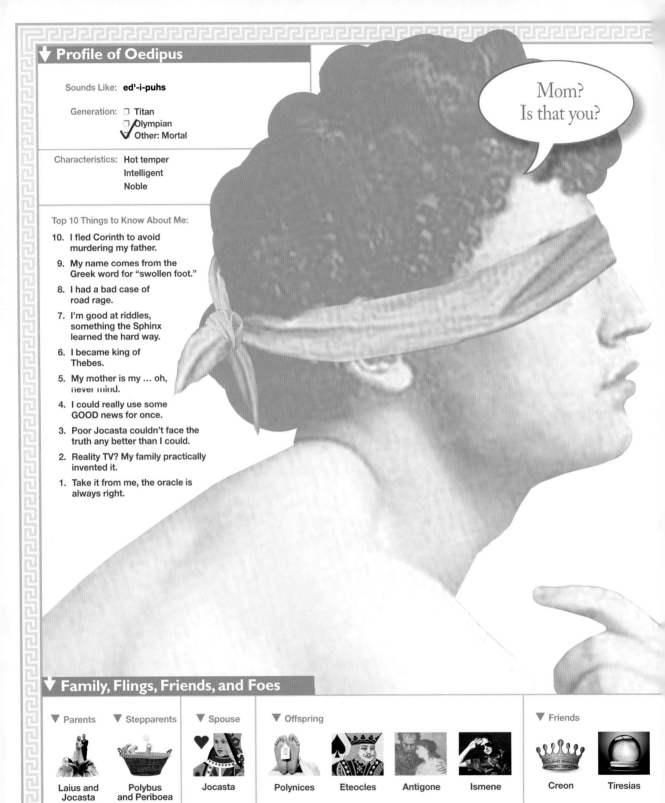

Profile of Oedipus

Sounds Like: ed'-i-puhs

Generation:
- ☐ Titan
- ☐ Olympian
- ☑ Other: Mortal

Characteristics: Hot temper
Intelligent
Noble

Top 10 Things to Know About Me:

10. I fled Corinth to avoid murdering my father.

9. My name comes from the Greek word for "swollen foot."

8. I had a bad case of road rage.

7. I'm good at riddles, something the Sphinx learned the hard way.

6. I became king of Thebes.

5. My mother is my ... oh, never mind.

4. I could really use some GOOD news for once.

3. Poor Jocasta couldn't face the truth any better than I could.

2. Reality TV? My family practically invented it.

1. Take it from me, the oracle is always right.

Mom?
Is that you?

Family, Flings, Friends, and Foes

▼ Parents	▼ Stepparents	▼ Spouse	▼ Offspring				▼ Friends	
Laius and Jocasta	Polybus and Periboea	Jocasta	Polynices	Eteocles	Antigone	Ismene	Creon	Tiresias

OEDIPUS

OEDIPUS EXPOSED!

THEBES—Shocking revelations about the secret life of Oedipus, king of Thebes, have rocked the country. Oracles today confirmed that the leader, a self-proclaimed riddle fanatic, is married to his own mother. In a gruesome twist, unidentified sources confirm that in a fit of road rage, Oedipus murdered the beloved king Laius, who was also his father. Palace employees, agreeing to talk off the record, claim they never suspected a thing.

Speaking to reporters clustered outside the city gates, Oedipus insisted he committed the horrible acts in ignorance. "I thought she looked familiar," he said, when asked how he met his wife.

REALITY CHECK

The Great Sphinx at Giza, Egypt, dates to about 3000 BCE. The body is in the shape of a lion and the head is that of a king wearing the royal headdress.

Want to know more: Go to: http://www.guardians.net/egypt/sphinx/

▼ Foes

DON'T ASK

Laius

The Sphinx

Who's your mama?

The Sphinx

OEDIPUS

"Anyone know any good riddles?"

MYTHLOPEDIA

Οιδιπους

IT'S GREEK TO ME

Oedipus's story is told in two plays by the Greek dramatist Sophocles: *Oedipus the King* and *Oedipus at Colonus*. The first is considered one of the greatest tragedies of world literature. In a third play, *Antigone*, Sophocles tells the tragic story of one of Oedipus's daughters.

Tragedy

OEDIPUS'S TROUBLES BEGIN AT HOME

A baby gets a break, but not for long.

The **Oracle** at Delphi had told King Laius and Queen Jocasta that their son Oedipus would kill his father and marry his mother. This **prophecy** came from the god Apollo, who spoke through the oracle. The royal pair was horrified by this awful prediction and hoped to avoid it. So they gave their firstborn to a shepherd and asked him to leave the baby outdoors to die. The baby's feet were then pierced and tied together (the name Oedipus means "swollen feet"). But the shepherd took pity on the tiny baby. Instead of leaving him to die in a field,

the shepherd gave him to a traveler on his way to the city of Corinth. There he was adopted by King Polybus and Queen Periboea.

My boy, I zink you haf some issues to verk out!

Sigmund Freud

BAD NEWS

Things go from bad to worse for Oedipus.

Oedipus was raised in Corinth as the son of King Polybus and Queen Periboea, never realizing that they were not his birth parents. When he was grown, Oedipus heard a rumor that he was not Polybus's son. He wanted to find out the truth, so he decided to travel to Delphi. There he asked the oracle who his parents actually were. But instead of answering Oedipus's question, the oracle delivered the same prophecy that Laius had heard so many years earlier: Oedipus would kill his father and marry his mother.

Oedipus was shocked by this prophecy and thought that it referred to King Polybus and Queen Periboea. He certainly did not want to harm the people who had raised and loved him, so he vowed to make sure the prophecy could not come true. He decided that if he did not return to Corinth, Polybus and Periboea would be safe. After all, he couldn't harm them if he never saw them again.

With this plan in mind, Oedipus left Delphi and started off for the city of Thebes.

Oracle

On the road, he met a man traveling in a **chariot**. The man was none other than Laius, his father. Of course, Oedipus did not recognize him.

Laius had four attendants with him, and they tried to force Oedipus from his path so that the chariot could go by. In the scuffle, Laius prodded Oedipus with his stick. Oedipus was arrogant and quick to anger. Furious at being prodded, he

killed Laius and three of the attendants. The fourth escaped to report the king's death to the people of Thebes.

"I just wanted to keep Mom and Dad safe."

RIDDLE OF THE SPHINX

Oedipus gets the right answer and wins the wrong wife.

The Sphinx

Oedipus

The murder of King Laius and his three attendants was not fully investigated because Thebes was then under siege by the Sphinx, a monster with the body of a winged lion and the breast and face of a woman. She sat on a rock outside the gates of Thebes and **devoured** everyone who failed to solve her riddle: "What creature walks on four legs in the morning, on two at noon, and on three in the evening?"

The people of Thebes were desperate until Oedipus came along and solved the riddle with the answer: "A human being. In infancy he crawls on all fours, in adulthood

he walks erect, in old age his third leg is a cane." When Oedipus gave the correct answer, the furious Sphinx hurled herself to her death.

Oedipus was welcomed to Thebes as a hero. The people offered him the throne and the hand in marriage of the widowed queen, Jocasta. Eventually, Oedipus and Jocasta had two sons, Polynices and Eteocles, and two daughters, Antigone and Ismene. The family lived happily … for a time.

What a combo!

Have you heard the one about the Sphinx?

The Great Sphinx at Giza

MYTHING LINK

The Sphinx is a hybrid, or mixed, creature, usually depicted with a lion's body and a human's upper torso and head. The sphinx as an art form also appeared in Egypt and Mesopotamia. It spread throughout the ancient world with variations in appearance and meaning.

MORE BAD NEWS

Oedipus can't handle the truth.

When Thebes was stricken by a plague, the people begged Oedipus for a solution. So he sent his brother-in-law Creon to Delphi to plead for the god Apollo's help. Apollo's **oracle** declared that the plague would go away when Laius's murderer was punished. Oedipus asked the **prophet** Tiresias to help find out the identity of the murderer. At first Tiresias refused to reveal the terrible secret. Finally he told Oedipus that he was Laius's murderer.

Oedipus leaving Thebes

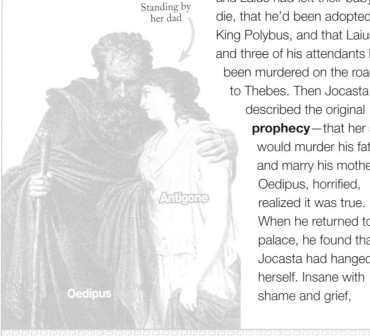
Standing by her dad
Antigone
Oedipus

Later, Jocasta confirmed what the prophet had said—that she and Laius had left their baby to die, that he'd been adopted by King Polybus, and that Laius and three of his attendants had been murdered on the road to Thebes. Then Jocasta described the original **prophecy**—that her son would murder his father and marry his mother. Oedipus, horrified, realized it was true. When he returned to the palace, he found that Jocasta had hanged herself. Insane with shame and grief,

Oedipus blinded himself. Creon took the throne and Oedipus was sent from Thebes. He later died near Athens.

REALITY CHECK

The Oracle at Delphi was located in the temple of Apollo, the god of prophecy. Mortals would go to the temple to ask questions about their fate. Even politicians consulted the oracle before making important decisions.

A Temple at Delphi

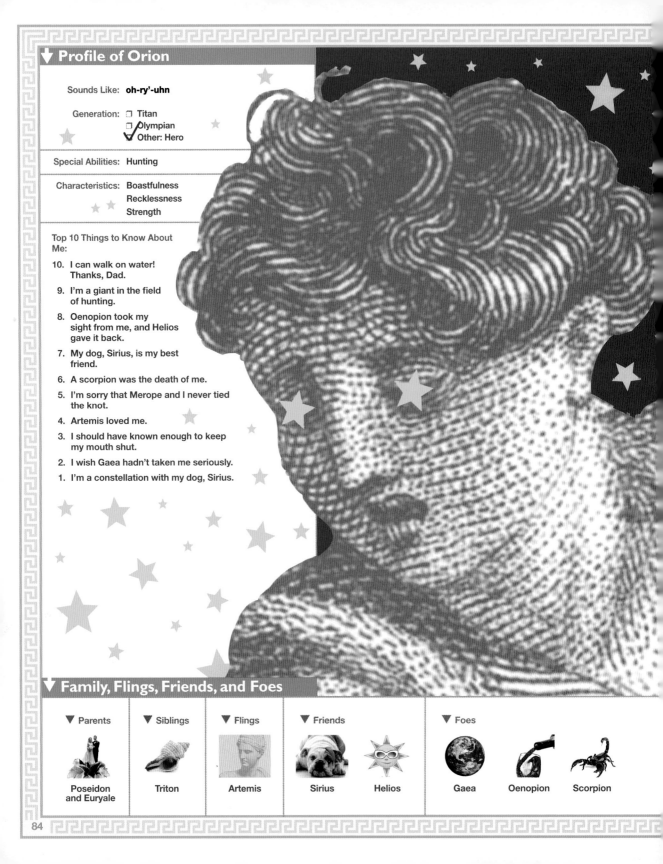

▼ Profile of Orion

Sounds Like: **oh-ry'-uhn**

Generation:
☐ Titan
☐ Olympian
☑ Other: Hero

Special Abilities: Hunting

Characteristics: Boastfulness
Recklessness
Strength

Top 10 Things to Know About Me:

10. I can walk on water! Thanks, Dad.

9. I'm a giant in the field of hunting.

8. Oenopion took my sight from me, and Helios gave it back.

7. My dog, Sirius, is my best friend.

6. A scorpion was the death of me.

5. I'm sorry that Merope and I never tied the knot.

4. Artemis loved me.

3. I should have known enough to keep my mouth shut.

2. I wish Gaea hadn't taken me seriously.

1. I'm a constellation with my dog, Sirius.

▼ Family, Flings, Friends, and Foes

▼ Parents	▼ Siblings	▼ Flings	▼ Friends		▼ Foes		
Poseidon and Euryale	Triton	Artemis	Sirius	Helios	Gaea	Oenopion	Scorpion

⭐RI⭐N

STAR POWER

Hellooooo! Hellooooo down there! Can you even hear me? I used to be one of the greats. My dad was a god! Artemis was my best friend! I could walk on water! Then Gaea got me good, sending that scorpion after me because I said I could kill every animal on Earth. Come on—I was just kidding! Can't you take a joke? Now I'm spending eternity as a constellation, and no one pays attention to me except to point at my belt. Some honor, Zeus!

Stick with me, kid, and I'll make you a star!

REALITY CHECK

In 2004, NASA unveiled the spacecraft *Orion* as part of its Constellation Program. The spacecraft is scheduled to take six astronauts to the International Space Station by 2014 and travel to the moon by 2020.

Want to know more? Go to: http://www.nasa.gov/mission_pages/constellation/orion/index.html

Artemis

Ὠρίων

★ ORION

"Everybody is a star!"

MYTHLOPEDIA

IT'S GREEK TO ME

Orion is one of a number of Greek mythological characters to be honored as a constellation, or group of stars that form a figure. Others include Heracles, Perseus, the Centaur, and the princess Andromeda. Animal constellations that have their roots in Greek mythology include Scorpius, the scorpion; Leo, the lion; Cygnus, the swan; Pegasus, the winged horse; and Draco, the dragon. Objects such as Lyra, the lyre, and Libra, the balance, are the basis for still other constellations.

"I don't care how it happened— I'm a star!"

ORION AND MEROPE

A great hunter is punished, then pitied.

The great hunter Orion was a giant of a man with magical powers. Because his father was Poseidon, god of the seas, Orion was able to walk on water as if it were solid ground. But Orion wasn't all good. He attacked Merope, the daughter of King Oenopion of Chios. The furious king punished Orion by blinding him.

Stumbling around, Orion made his way to Lemnos, the home of the Olympian god Hephaestus, a skilled craftsman and **blacksmith**. Hephaestus took pity on the blind hunter and sent him to see Helios, the sun god. Helios restored Orion's sight with his life-giving sun rays.

MYTHING LINK

Helios, the Greek sun god, had a big job. Every day, driving his golden **chariot**, he pulled the sun across the sky from his palace in the east to another palace in the west. Then every night he sailed back to the east in a golden boat. The worship of Helios was centered on the Isle of Rhodes. There stood a 105-foot-tall bronze statue of Helios, known as the Colossus of Rhodes. One of the Seven Wonders of the Ancient World, the statue was destroyed by an earthquake in 226 BCE.

Boy, was he a sight for sore eyes!

Helios

THE DEATH OF ORION, TAKE TWO

Artemis idolizes Orion, but she ends up killing him.

In another version of Orion's story, the god Apollo was jealous that his sister Artemis loved Orion. One day Apollo saw Orion swimming in the water with just his head sticking up. He challenged Artemis to hit the "mark" in the water with her bow and arrow. Not knowing it was Orion, Artemis took the challenge and killed the man she loved. When she realized what she'd done, she was horrified. Apollo regretted his trick. To show his sister he was sorry, he turned Orion into a constellation of stars and placed him in the heavens.

THE DEATH OF ORION

Orion pays the price for boasting.

Orion's troubles didn't end with the princess Merope. Artemis, goddess of the hunt, fell in love with him. One day she and her mother, Leto, went hunting with Orion. During the hunt, Orion boasted that he could kill every beast on Earth. Gaea, the earth goddess, heard him and decided to punish him for saying such a thing. She sent a giant scorpion that stung and killed Orion. Artemis was so saddened by his death that she pleaded with Zeus to place him in the heavens as a constellation. Zeus did so, but also made a constellation of the scorpion that had killed him. His beloved dog, Sirius, became part of a constellation as well.

REALITY CHECK

With pincers and a stinger, scorpions have a frightening appearance. Like spiders, they are arachnids, not insects. These creatures have been around for more than 420 million years. One scorpion fossil dating that far back was more than three feet long!

Want to know more? Go to: www.sandiegozoo.org

MYTHING LINK

Whether Orion was shot by an arrow or stung by a scorpion, the ending of this myth is the same—he was killed. Like the death of Orion, many myths have more than one version of how something happened. The variations came about because these tales were told at different times in history and by many different storytellers, such as Hesiod, Homer, Aeschuylus, Euripedes, and Sophocles.

Profile of Orpheus

Sounds Like: or'-fee-uhs

Generation: ☐ Titan
☐ Olympian
☑ Other: Mortal

Special Abilities: Music

Characteristics: Creativity
Romantic nature
Thoughtfulness

Attributes: Lyre

I can't live without youuuuu …

Top 10 Things to Know About Me:

10. I'm the original rock star.

9. My mother was a Muse, so it's no wonder I'm creative.

8. Eurydice was the love of my life.

7. I found out that the Underworld deserves its reputation.

6. I can put fierce dogs to sleep with my music.

5. Hades and Persephone turned to putty when they heard me play.

4. Just one little peek and my wife was gone for good.

3. I lost my head when the Maenads got hold of me.

2. Heard of talking heads? Mine was a singing head.

1. My lyre can be seen up in the night sky.

Family, Flings, Friends, and Foes

▼ Parents	▼ Spouse	▼ Offspring	▼ Sibling	▼ Friend	▼ Foes	
Apollo and Calliope	Eurydice	Musaeus	Aristaeus	Jason	Dionysus	The Maenads

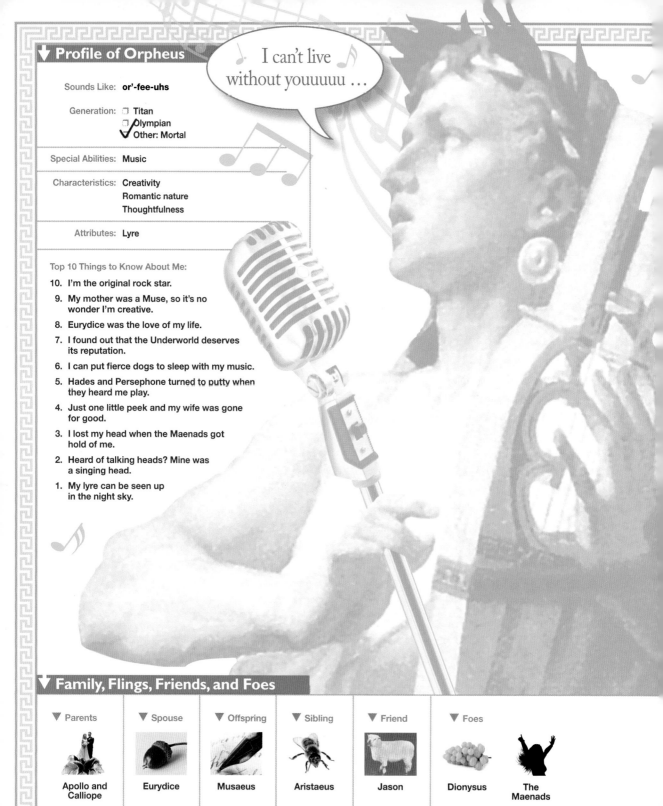

ORPHEUS

♪ SINGING THE BLUES

Hey, lonely lovers, thanks for tuning in to K-SAD, home of the saddest love songs on the air. DJ Orpheus here, set to spin some songs that will break your heart—if it hasn't been broken already. Let's bring it down with a new tune by yours truly, about the death of my wife, Eurydice, my trip to the Underworld to save her, and how I lost her all over again. This is a big shout-out to you, E.

REALITY CHECK

The lyre was a popular musical instrument in ancient Greece. It looked something like a small harp. The lyre was supposedly invented by Hermes, messenger of the gods, and it was one of Apollo's symbols. The modern words *lyric* and *lyrical* come from *lyre*.

Want to know more? Go to:
http://www.historyforkids.org/ learn/greeks/art/music/

ORPHEUS

"I'd like to sing you a sad song!"

MYTHOPEDIA

Ορφευς

IT'S GREEK TO ME

Tartarus, a region of the Underworld, was a prison beneath the earth where the Titans, an early group of **immortals**, were banished by their children, the Olympians. The **Underworld** was ruled by Hades, its king, and his queen, Persephone. It was also known as the House of Hades, or simply Hades. Cerberus, a fierce, three-headed dog, guarded the gates of Hades, keeping the dead from leaving.

"I did not look,
I just peeked."

ORPHEUS AND EURYDICE

Orpheus takes a peek and loses his lady.

Orpheus's mother, Calliope, was one of the nine Muses of the arts. When Orpheus was a boy, his father, Apollo, the god of music, gave him a little golden **lyre** and taught him to play it. By the time he grew up, Orpheus was the greatest musician in all of Greece. The beautiful music he made charmed the animals and made the trees dance. Stones followed him when he played, and rivers stopped running to listen.

Eurydice

Cerberus

Orpheus

Do NOT look back!

Orpheus fell madly in love with the **nymph** Eurydice. They married and were very happy together. Then one day, Orpheus's stepbrother, Aristaeus, attacked Eurydice. She fled from him into the woods, where she was bitten on the heel by a poisonous snake and died.

Orpheus was heartbroken. From then on, he played and sang only sad songs. Finally, the mighty god Zeus gave Orpheus permission to try to get Eurydice back from Hades and Persephone, the king and queen of the Underworld.

Orpheus traveled to the gates of the Underworld, where he was met by the three-headed watchdog, Cerberus. He strummed his lyre, and his beautiful music lulled Cerberus to sleep.

Continuing on, Orpheus was next met by Hades and Persephone. They would have refused his request, but his sorrowful music melted their cold hearts. So they gave him permission to take Eurydice back to the land of the living, with one catch: On the way out of the Underworld, Orpheus had to walk in front of Eurydice. He couldn't look at her until they were back on Earth. Not even a peek!

Carefully Orpheus made his way through the Underworld with Eurydice following behind—he hoped. No, he was sure. Well, pretty sure. Almost 100 percent sure. As they neared the entrance, Orpheus took a quick glance—just a little peek—at his wife. As he did, Eurydice vanished and was lost to him forever.

THE DEATH OF ORPHEUS

You can't keep a good musician down—for long.

After losing his wife for a second time, Orpheus wandered into the forest, where he played **mournful** songs on his lyre. Many women were attracted to him for his music but he would have nothing to do with them. The Maenads, nymphs who worshipped the god Dionysus, took Orpheus's rejection of them personally and tore him to pieces with their bare hands. They threw his head into the River Hebrus, where it was said to cry Eurydice's name as it floated downstream into the sea and on to the island of Lesbos. Orpheus's lyre was placed in the heavens as the constellation Lyra.

MYTHING LINK

Dionysus was the god of fertility, poetry, song, and wine making. The Maenads were his followers, and many festivals were held in his honor. One of the most interesting stories about Dionysus involves his birth. When his mother, Semele, died before he was born, his father, Zeus, rescued the unborn Dionysus and sewed him into his own thigh. Dionysus kept growing there until he was ready to be born!

Lost his head!

Orpheus

Maenad

Sounds Like: **pan-dohr'-uh**

Aliases: **Anesidora**

Generation: ☐ Titan
☐ Olympian
☑ Other: Mortal

Characteristics: Allure
Beauty
Curiosity

*For me?
You shouldn't have!*

Top 10 Things to Know About Me:

10. I was the first woman in the world. Talk about being special!

9. Hephaestus, the god of crafts, made me out of clay.

8. The gods and goddesses gave me all the charm and beauty a girl could want.

7. Epimetheus married me; he said I was a "gift."

6. I was made as a *punishment*? What is *that* supposed to mean?

5. Zeus gave me a present and told me not to open it. Yeah, right!

4. I really don't like taking the blame for all the world's ills.

3. People still talk about "Pandora's box" every time unforeseen trouble crops up.

2. Let me set the record straight. It was a jar, not a box!

1. I don't want you to worry. There's always hope.

**DO NOT OPEN
UNTIL XMAS
EVER**

▼ Family, Flings, Friends, and Foes

▼ Parents	▼ Spouse	▼ Offspring	▼ Friends		
Hephaestus	Epimetheus	Pyrrha	 Zeus	 Aphrodite	 Athena

PANDORA

A WORLD OF TROUBLE

Hey humans, I owe you a super-big apology! If I'd known what was in that jar, I never would have opened it! Seriously! If Zeus gave *you* a present, you'd want to open it, right? Nobody told me it was full of trouble for humans. What kind of present is that, anyway? You should blame Zeus, not me! Anyway, I'm really sorry. You can stop calling me a punishment for all humankind now. It was a simple mistake! Can't you forgive and forget?

REALITY CHECK

Pandora is the name of the planet Saturn's fourth moon. It was discovered in 1980 from photographs taken by *Voyager I*, a space probe. Pandora is 52 miles in diameter. It lies near Saturn's third moon, Prometheus.

Want to know more? Go to: http://www.nineplanets.org/pandora.html

You don't know the half of it!

▼ Foes

Hermes   **Prometheus**

Zeus

PANDORA

"Uh-oh."

MYTHLOPEDIA

Πανδωρα

IT'S GREEK TO ME

The original Greek myth calls it "Pandora's jar." So how did the jar come to be called a box? The container Pandora opened was a *pithos*, a large jar used in ancient Greece to store oil, wine, or grain. When the sixteenth-century Dutch author Erasmus was translating the myth into Latin, he translated the Greek word *pithos* into the Latin word *pyxis*, which means "box." From then on, the myth was known as "Pandora's box."

"Talk about opening a can of worms ..."

PANDORA'S GIFTS

Zeus gives humankind the first woman.

Zeus, ruler of the gods, was furious. Prometheus had stolen fire from the gods and taken it to humans—against Zeus's strict orders! Zeus punished Prometheus by chaining him to a rock and having an eagle come every day to eat his liver. The liver would grow back at night, and the eagle would return the next day to eat it again. This went

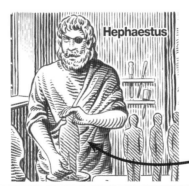

Hephaestus

One woman coming up!

on until Prometheus was rescued by Heracles, a son of Zeus, 13 generations later.

Zeus wanted to punish humankind, too. So he ordered the god Hephaestus, a master craftsman and **blacksmith**, to mold a woman out of clay. She was named Pandora, which means "all gifts." The name certainly fit! The Olympian gods and goddesses gave Pandora many gifts. From Aphrodite she received beauty; from Athena, skills in the arts; and from Hermes, cunning, deceit, and speech. Finally, she was given a sealed jar and delivered to Epimetheus.

Oops.

Pandora

Heap o' trouble

GREED

HATE

WAR

PANDORA'S JAR

Pandora opens a jar full of troubles.

Zeus, playing matchmaker, sent Pandora to Epimetheus, Prometheus's brother, who married her even though he'd been warned by Prometheus not to accept gifts from Zeus.

In time, Pandora and Epimetheus removed the lid of the jar to see what was inside.

Out flew all the troubles, evils, and sickness in the world. Quickly Pandora replaced the lid, leaving only hope inside the jar. Despite all the troubles that humankind would now suffer, there would always be hope.

REALITY CHECK
The Boxes, a novel by William Sleator, is based on the myth of Pandora's jar. In the novel, a girl named Annie opens one of two boxes left her by her uncle, who has told her not to open them. Out of the box comes something terrible: a crab-like creature that quickly multiplies.

AFTER THE FLOOD

Pandora's daughter repopulates the earth.

Epimetheus and Pandora had a daughter named Pyrrha. Pyrrha grew up and married Deucalion, a son of Prometheus. When Zeus sent a great flood to punish humankind for its wickedness, Pyrrha and Deucalion, saved in an ark, were the only survivors. After the floodwaters receded, an **oracle** instructed them to create a new race of humans by casting the bones of their mother behind them. Deucalion thought that by "bones" the oracle meant they should throw the stones of their common parent, the earth, so that's what they did. As they cast the stones behind them, those thrown by Deucalion became men, and those thrown by Pyrrha became women.

pile of stones

PANDORA'S BAD

Pandora just couldn't wait to open her present from Zeus. She should have known better!

Sounds Like: pahr'-iss

Generation: ☐ Titan
☐ Olympian
✓ Other: Mortal

Characteristics: Athleticism
Cowardice
Dishonorableness
Fairness
Weakness

Attributes: Bow and arrow
Burning torch

You're the winner, Aphrodite!

Top 10 Things to Know About Me:

10. I wasn't exactly raised by wolves—but my adopted mom was a real bear!

9. I'm a pretty handsome guy, if I do say so myself.

8. Sorry that my crush on Helen left Troy a wreck!

7. How come my brother Hector got to be the brave one, and everyone thinks I'm a big coward? No fair!

6. Before I was born, my mom dreamed that I'd destroy Troy. Looks like dreams really do come true.

5. I was a real pro at arranging bullfights, and I was always fair at declaring the winner. Just ask Ares, who tried to trick me.

4. Even though I was born a prince, I was raised a commoner.

3. Zeus picked me to judge the ultimate goddess beauty contest. Tough job, but somebody's got to do it.

2. Who cares if Helen's already married? I'm a prince!

1. I accidentally started the Trojan War. Oops— my bad!

Family, Flings, Friends, and Foes

▼ Parents

Priam and Hecuba

▼ Spouses

Oenone

Helen of Troy

▼ Siblings

Cassandra

Hector

Laodice

Polydorus

Helenus

PARIS

JUDGMENT DAY

My family has never appreciated me. Never! Before I was born, my mom dreamed I would destroy Troy. My dad ordered me to be left on a hillside to die (thanks, Pops). Even my brother Hector thinks he's some big hero next to me. Well, riddle me this, family—did Zeus pick any of *you* to choose the fairest goddess of them all? No? Oh, *too bad*, because he thinks I'm *just* the man for the job!

Have I got a girl for you!

Aphrodite

REALITY CHECK

Beauty pageants are held worldwide, with an estimated 700,000 annual U.S. contests attracting 3–4 million entrants. Prizes can include cars and college scholarships. Contestants are judged on their beauty, and sometimes on other categories such as talent and poise.

Want to know more? Go to: http://www.missamerica.org

▼ Friends

Aphrodite   Agalaeus   The Trojans

▼ Foes

Ares   Menelaus   Hera   Athena   The Greeks

PARIS

"All's fair in love and war."

MYTH-LOPEDIA

Παρις

IT'S GREEK TO ME

Seers, or prophets, played an important role in Greek mythology. They interpreted dreams and foretold the future. Tiresias, who was given the gift of foresight by Zeus, was one of the best known seers. He predicted that Narcissus would live only if he did not see his own image. Even after his death, Tiresias could still foresee the future. He predicted that Odysseus would have a difficult journey back to Ithaca, and he was certainly right! Other notable seers included Phineus and Calchas.

> "Who is the fairest of them all? I know!"

Hey! That's my baby!

BAD OMEN BEFORE BIRTH

Paris's mom gets a glimpse of the trouble her kid will cause.

King Priam and Queen Hecuba had many children—but the night before the birth of her second son, Paris, Hecuba had a terrible nightmare. She dreamed that she gave birth to a torch that burned down the entire city of Troy! A seer interpreted the dream to mean that Hecuba's unborn child would cause Troy's destruction. So, with heavy hearts, Priam and Hecuba ordered a shepherd to abandon newborn Paris on a hillside, where the baby would die of exposure and no longer pose a threat to Troy. But a female bear cared for the infant, keeping him alive until the shepherd decided to secretly raise Paris as his own son. Paris grew up never knowing that he was royalty— or that the people he called his parents weren't biologically related to him. Many years later, at an athletic event, his sister Cassandra recognized him, and he was welcomed back into the royal family of Troy.

Paris

shepherds

Hecuba

THE TROJAN WAR

Paris kidnaps a beauty and starts a war.

When King Priam's sister was kidnapped by Heracles, Paris led the rescue mission. Menelaus, king of Sparta, offered his hospitality to Paris on the trip. Menelaus was married to Helen, the most beautiful woman in the world. Paris took one look at her and claimed his prize for naming Aphrodite winner of the beauty contest: He kidnapped Helen and took her to Troy.

Menelaus couldn't let Helen go without a fight. He led the Greek army to Troy to retrieve her. In the war that lasted ten years, many heroes emerged. Paris, however, wasn't one of them. He preferred to stay out of harm's way and shoot arrows. With Apollo's help, Paris shot and killed the Greek hero Achilles. Paris was finally killed by a poisoned arrow shot by Heracles' armor-bearer. Troy was ultimately destroyed— and Queen Hecuba's prophetic dream about her son's destiny came true.

THE JUDGMENT OF PARIS

Zeus picks Paris to judge the ultimate beauty contest.

All the **deities** were invited to the marriage of Poleus and Thetis—except for one: Eris, the goddess of **discord**. After all, discord doesn't belong at a wedding. But Eris was determined to get revenge for the slight. At the reception, she threw a golden apple marked "For the most beautiful" into the crowd. Three goddesses—Hera, Athena, and Aphrodite—fell right into Eris's trap. They immediately began to argue over who the apple was really meant for—and which goddess was the most beautiful. Zeus didn't want to choose, so he gave the job to Paris. Each goddess promised Paris a great prize in return for his vote: Hera promised him wealth and power; Athena offered him wisdom and victory in war; and Aphrodite promised him the most beautiful woman in the world, Helen of Troy. Paris immediately declared Aphrodite the winner, making some powerful enemies in Hera and Athena. What Paris didn't know at the time was that his choice would lead to the Trojan War— and his own untimely death.

▼ Profile of Perseus

Sounds Like: **pur'-see-uhs**

Generation: ☐ Titan
☐ Olympian
☑ Other: Hero

Characteristics: Bravery
Resourcefulness

Attributes: Invisibility helmet
Reflective shield
Winged sandals

Top 10 Things to Know About Me:

10. I was the very first Greek hero of myth.

9. With Zeus for a father, I had to amount to something.

8. I can't understand why my own grandfather would want me dead.

7. I wonder how I ever ended up with Polydectes for a stepfather.

6. My accessories have made me quite the successful monster slayer.

5. I "reflected" on Medusa before I cut off her ugly head.

4. After what I went through with Medusa, killing the sea monster Ceto was a piece of cake.

3. Polydectes already had a heart of stone. I just finished the job.

2. I yelled "Duck!" when I threw the discus, but I guess Grandpa didn't hear me.

1. Both my wife, Andromeda, and I ended up as constellations.

> Ding-dong, the witch is dead!

▼ Family, Flings, Friends, and Foes

▼ Parents	▼ Grandfather	▼ Spouse	▼ Offspring					
Zeus and Danaë	Acrisius	Andromeda	Perses	Alcaeus	Heleus	Mestor	Sthenelus	Electryon

PERSEUS

SPORTING HERO

REPORTER: I'm coming to you live from Thessaly's athletic games. With me is Perseus, an inspiring hero.

PERSEUS: I don't really consider myself a hero. I killed Medusa just to save my mom from an awful marriage. Yeah, I had a rough start, but Grandpa, if you're out there—I forgive you.

REPORTER: You're competing in your first ever discus event. Nervous?

PERSEUS: A little. I can throw far but I'm not as accurate as I'd like to be.

Medusa

So not funny.

▼ Foes

Cynurus

Gorgophone

Autochthoe

Hermes

Athena

Hades

Acrisius

Medusa

Polydectes

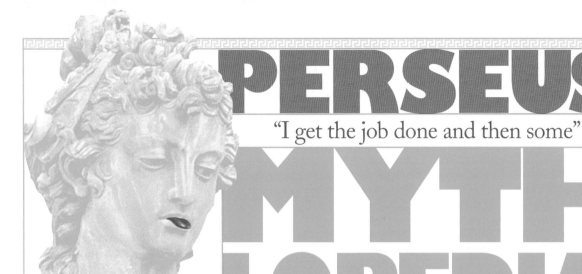

PERSEUS

"I get the job done and then some"

MYTHLOPEDIA

Περσευς

IT'S GREEK TO ME

The Greeks believed in the power of the Gorgons, three horrifying sisters with snakes in place of hair, wings, bronze claws, and teeth like boars' tusks. They painted Gorgons' faces on their shields and armor to frighten their enemies in battle. The terrifying sight was thought to distract an enemy long enough for the Greek with the shield to kill him.

"Acrisius just couldn't handle the truth!"

ALL WASHED UP

Perseus rides the waves.

An **oracle** told King Acrisius that his daughter Danaë would have a son who would one day kill him. Acrisius locked Danaë in an underground chamber so she'd never marry. But the mighty god Zeus was in love with Danaë. He got past Danaë's father by turning himself into a shower of gold and pouring into Danaë's chamber. Soon Zeus and Danaë were the proud parents of a son, Perseus.

Worried about what the oracle had said, Acrisius put his daughter and grandson in a wooden chest and cast them out to sea. The chest washed up on the shores of Seriphos, where King Polydectes took them in and Perseus grew up.

This is no way to travel!

Mom, are we there yet?

GOING AFTER A MONSTER

A shiny shield saves Perseus.

Polydectes loved Perseus's mother, Danaë, but she wanted nothing to do with him. The evil king figured that if he got Perseus out of the way, Danaë might consider marrying him. So Polydectes sent Perseus on a quest to bring back the head of Medusa, one of the three horrible Gorgon sisters. These hideous monsters had wings, bronze claws, snakes coming out of their heads instead of hair, and faces that turned anyone who looked at them to stone.

The task seemed impossible, but several gods sent gifts to help Perseus. Speedy Hermes gave him his winged sandals; Hades, king of the **Underworld**, gave him his helmet of invisibility; and the warrior goddess Athena offered her reflecting shield.

As Perseus approached Medusa, he held Athena's shield in front of him, looking at Medusa's reflection rather than directly at her so she couldn't turn him to stone. Then he cut off her head with a sword. To escape Medusa's sisters, Perseus put on the helmet of invisibility. The two Gorgons couldn't see him, and he escaped.

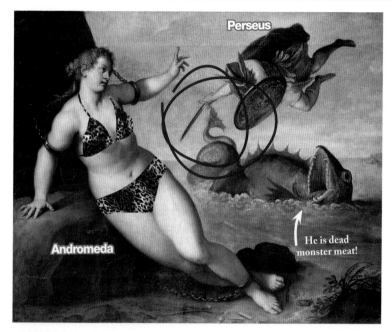

Perseus

Andromeda

He is dead monster meat!

PERSEUS'S NEW POWER

The power to turn things—and people—to stone comes in handy.

Possession of Medusa's head gave Perseus the power to turn anything to stone. On his way home, he turned the mighty Titan Atlas into a mountain and rescued the beautiful princess Andromeda from a sea monster by transforming the beast into a rock. He and Andromeda were later married.

After returning to Seriphos, Perseus saved his mother from King Polydectes by revealing the head of Medusa and turning the

king to stone. He then gave Medusa's head to Athena, who placed it on her shield. Perseus followed his grandfather Acrisius to Thessaly, where he had gone to hide. There, Perseus took part in an athletic contest and accidentally killed his grandfather with a discus. Once again, the oracle's prophecy was fulfilled.

REALITY CHECK

The story of Perseus was excitingly retold in the 1981 film *Clash of the Titans*. It featured special effects by master animator Ray Harryhausen. The all-star cast featured Harry Hamlin as Perseus and Laurence Olivier as Zeus.

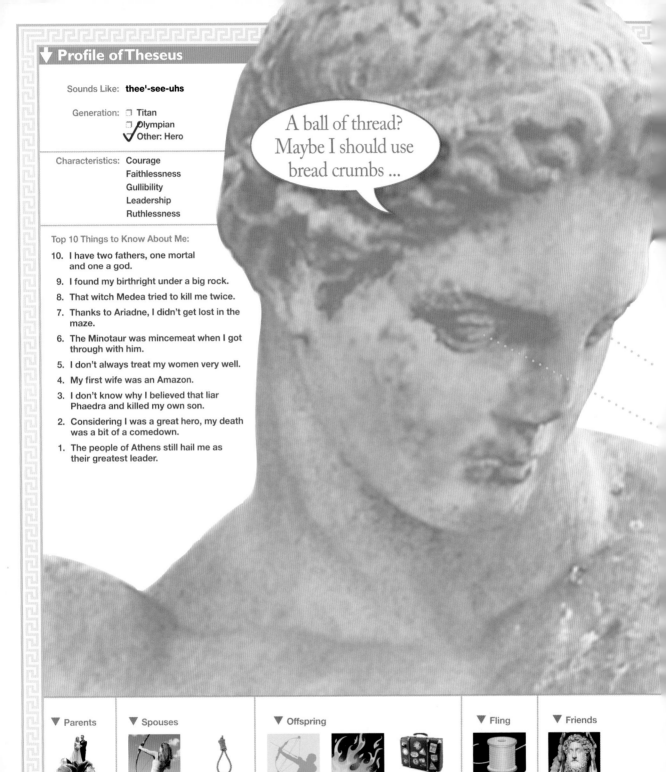

▼ Profile of Theseus

Sounds Like: thee'-see-uhs

Generation: ☐ Titan
☐ Olympian
✓ Other: Hero

Characteristics: Courage
Faithlessness
Gullibility
Leadership
Ruthlessness

A ball of thread? Maybe I should use bread crumbs ...

Top 10 Things to Know About Me:

10. I have two fathers, one mortal and one a god.

9. I found my birthright under a big rock.

8. That witch Medea tried to kill me twice.

7. Thanks to Ariadne, I didn't get lost in the maze.

6. The Minotaur was mincemeat when I got through with him.

5. I don't always treat my women very well.

4. My first wife was an Amazon.

3. I don't know why I believed that liar Phaedra and killed my own son.

2. Considering I was a great hero, my death was a bit of a comedown.

1. The people of Athens still hail me as their greatest leader.

▼ Parents	▼ Spouses		▼ Offspring			▼ Fling	▼ Friends
Aegeus or Poseidon and Aethra	Hippolyte	Phaedra	Hippolytus	Demophon	Acamas	Ariadne	Heracles

THESEUS

A ROYAL PAIN

So I was all, yeah, whatever, send me to the Minotaur. Killing that bull-headed freakshow was no big deal. I was all, *take that*! And *that*! You know, I'm the only person in the history of the world to get out of that labyrinth alive. Did I mention I'm a prince of Athens? Have you been talking to Ariadne? Don't believe a word she says. Yeah, she gave me that ball of thread but we drifted apart. So what if I left her on a desert island? So sue me. I'm a hero, remember?

Doesn't matter. You'll never get out!

REALITY CHECK

The famous labyrinth of King Minos has given its name to any complicated maze that a person can get lost in. Outdoor garden mazes have paths lined with high hedges that lead eventually to a center area. They were especially popular in England in the 1600s and 1700s.

Want to know more? Go to: http://www.mazes.org.uk/

The Minotaur

▼ Foes

Oedipus

Plrithous

King Minos

The Minotaur

The Amazons

Medea

THESEUS

"Don't give me any bull!"

MYTHLOPEDIA

Θησευς

IT'S GREEK TO ME

Animal sacrifice to the gods was a common practice among the Greeks. The animals were offered as gifts to the gods in return for their favors. The animals were often burned on an altar in a temple, and the smoke from the burnt offering would rise to the heavens.

temple

ROLL THE ROCK

Theseus finds buried treasure.
When Aethra, a princess of Troezen, gave birth to Theseus, she wasn't sure if his father was King Aegeus of Athens or the god of the sea, Poseidon. Before Aegeus left Troezen and returned to Athens, he buried his sandals and sword under a huge rock. He told Aethra that if she gave birth to a son who was manly enough, that son would be able to move the rock one day. When that happened, Aethra was to send her son to Athens with the sandals and sword, so that Aegeus would recognize him.

As he was growing up, Theseus shared both his earthly father's humanity and his godly father's powers. Then when he grew strong enough to move the rock, Theseus took the sandals and sword his father had left. With this proof of his identity in hand, he went to Athens to claim his **birthright** as Aegeus's son.

rock

Theseus

sword & sandals

Well, lookie here!

Medea tried everything!

hidden sandals

poison wine

bull sacrifice

THESEUS AND MEDEA

A sorceress tries to outdo a hero.

At first Aegeus did not realize that Theseus was his son. But Aegeus's new wife, the **sorceress** Medea, recognized Theseus, and she wanted to protect the kingship for her own child by Aegeus. Encouraged by Medea, Aegeus sent Theseus on a quest to capture the wild Marathonian bull. Theseus captured the bull, brought it back to the palace, and sacrificed it to the god Apollo.

Medea still wanted to get Theseus out of the way, so she poisoned a cup of wine and urged Aegeus to give it to Theseus. Just as he was about to hand his son the drink, Aegeus recognized his sandals and sword and knew Theseus was his son. He took the cup from Theseus's hand, welcomed him home, and sent Medea into **exile**.

REALITY CHECK

Theseus has had a long afterlife in world literature. He turns up in one of Geoffrey Chaucer's *Canterbury Tales* and in William Shakespeare's comedy *A Midsummer Night's Dream*. In Shakespeare's play, Theseus, referred to as the Duke of Athens, is engaged to be married to Hippolyta, Queen of the Amazons.

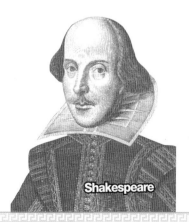

Shakespeare

THESEUS STEPS UP

A hero heads off to Crete.

Athens had been defeated in a war by King Minos of Crete. As a **tribute**, Minos made Aegeus, the king of Athens, send seven young men and seven young women to Crete every year. The young people were fed to the Minotaur, a half-man, half-bull monster that lived in a **labyrinth**, or maze.

As the deadline approached for sending the next batch of young people to their certain death, Theseus told his father that he would go, too. He planned to kill the Minotaur. Aegeus reluctantly agreed. But he made his son promise that if he survived his encounter with the bullish beast, he would hoist a white sail on his ship as he returned home. If he died, the crew was to leave the usual black sail in place. With that promise, the brave Theseus set sail for Crete.

AN AMAZING RESCUE

A princess and a hero team up.

When Theseus arrived in Crete to kill the Minotaur, King Minos's daughter Ariadne fell in love with the courageous hero. Theseus told Ariadne about his mission, and the clever princess promised to help him if he would marry her and take her to Athens. Theseus agreed, so Ariadne gave him a sword and a ball of thread. She explained that he was to unwind the thread behind him as he made his way into the labyrinth.

Once he had killed the Minotaur with the sword, he would be able to follow the thread and find his way out of the maze.

Finally the day came for Theseus and the other youths to enter the Minotaur's **labyrinth**. Theseus made his way through the walls of the maze toward the sleeping Minotaur, unwinding the thread along the way. When he reached the monster, he killed it with the sword. Then Theseus found his way out, following the trail he had left.

Minotaur

MISSION ACCOMPLISHED

Theseus leaves his love behInd.

Theseus and Ariadne set sail for Athens, joined by the youths the hero had saved from being eaten by the Minotaur. But along the way, Theseus abandoned Ariadne on the island of Naxos. This enraged the goddess of love, Aphrodite, so she punished Theseus by making him forget his promise to hoist a white sail if he had conquered the Minotaur.

Meanwhile, King Aegeus was keeping watch for his son's return. When he saw the ship appear under a black sail, he took it as a sign that his son was dead, and threw himself into the sea, where he drowned. Theseus sadly assumed his father's crown as king of Athens.

Theseus

Minotaur

THESEUS AND PHAEDRA

It's payback time.

A tribe of female warriors, the Amazons, had attacked Athens. They were defeated by Theseus, who took the Amazon Antiope (some versions of the story say Hippolyte) as his wife. The two soon had a son, Hippolytus. Time went by, and Theseus left Antiope to marry Phaedra, another daughter of King Minos. Soon Phaedra grew bored with Theseus and fell in love with Hippolytus. A loyal son, Hippolytus refused to betray his father and he rejected Phaedra's advances. Infuriated at being rejected, Phaedra hanged herself, but she left a note for Theseus claiming that Hippolytus had tried to attack her. Theseus, believing the note, called on the mighty Poseidon, the god of the sea, to kill Hippolytus. Poseidon sent a sea monster to frighten the horses that pulled Hippolytus's **chariot**, and the youth was dragged to his death.

Phaedra's noose

Sea monster

A FAILED QUEST

Theseus can't catch a break.

After Phaedra's death, Theseus wanted to marry again. He and his friend Pirithous decided that they would each marry a daughter of Zeus, king of the gods. Pirithous helped Theseus kidnap Helen of Troy, a beautiful princess. In return, Theseus helped Pirithous try to kidnap Persephone, queen of the **Underworld**. But their plan was foiled by Hades, god of the Underworld. As punishment, Hades bound the two friends to benches by chains from which they could not escape. Theseus was finally rescued by Heracles, who was in the Underworld trying to complete the last of his twelve labors. But Pirithous was not so lucky; he remained in the Underworld forever.

Theseus's plan to marry was destined to failure. On his return to Athens, he learned that Helen had been rescued by her brothers Castor and Pollux.

The one-time hero soon fell out of favor with the Athenians, and he left to visit his friend Lycomedes in Skyros for **refuge**. But fearing that Theseus would try to take over his throne, Lycomedes pushed him off a cliff to his death.

That is no way to treat a friend!

Theseus

Lycomedes

113

FAMILY TREE

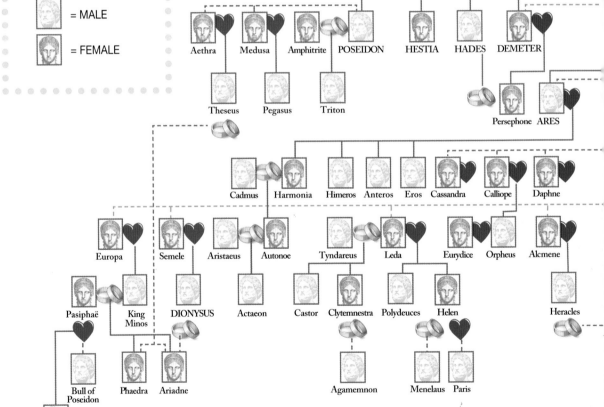

Aethra · Medusa · Amphitrite · POSEIDON · HESTIA · HADES · DEMETER

Theseus · Pegasus · Triton · Persephone · ARES

Cadmus · Harmonia · Himeros · Anteros · Eros · Cassandra · Calliope · Daphne

Europa · Semele · Aristaeus · Autonoe · Tyndareus · Leda · Eurydice · Orpheus · Alcmene

Pasiphaë · King Minos · DIONYSUS · Actaeon · Castor · Clytemnestra · Polydeuces · Helen · Heracles

Bull of Poseidon · Phaedra · Ariadne · Agamemnon · Menelaus · Paris

Minotaur

114

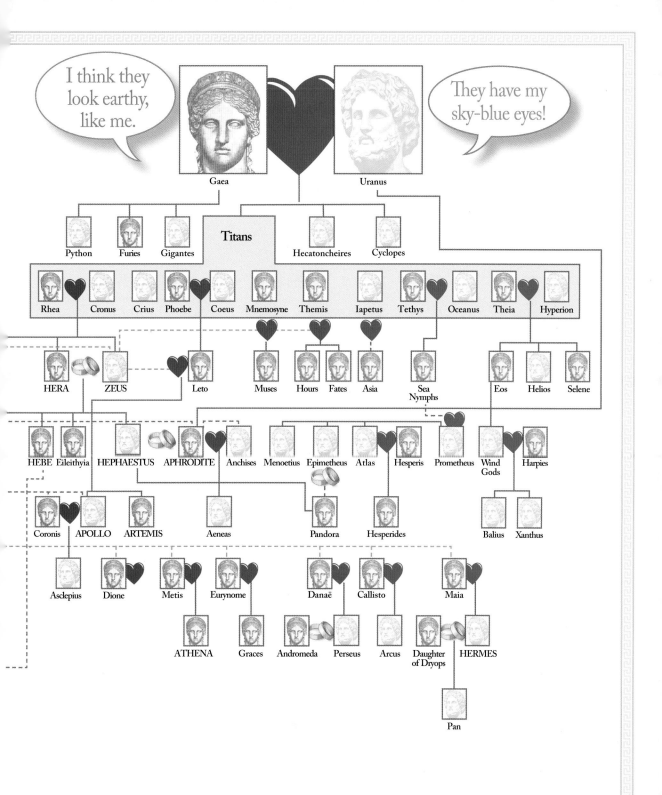

GLOSSARY

archeologist   a scientist who studies the remains of past human life and culture

Argonauts   the crew that traveled with the hero Jason onboard the *Argo*

begrudgingly   reluctantly

birthright   a privilege, right, or possession that someone is entitled to by birth

blacksmith   a worker who shapes metal into useful objects

buffeted   battered; struck forcefully

Centaur   a creature with the head and upper body of a human and the legs and lower body of a horse

chariot   a two-wheeled vehicle drawn by horses

cuirass   armor that protects the chest and back

deities   gods or goddesses

demigod   a child born to a human being and a god

devoured   ate greedily

discord   conflict or strong disagreement

epic   a long poem that tells the story of a hero

exile   to force someone to leave his or her country and live elsewhere

Golden Fleece   the fleece of a golden ram, which was the object of the Argonauts' quest

immortal   living forever

incessant   continuing without interruption

intervene   step in to help

invincible   incapable of being conquered

labyrinth   a maze, or complicated, confusing arrangement of paths

lyre   a U-shaped stringed instrument related to the harp

mortal   a human being; subject to death

mournful	expressing sadness or sorrow
nymph	a female spirit associated with nature
oracle	a priestess or priest who communicated the response of a god to a questioner.
premonition	a warning of something to come
promontories	land masses that project into a body of water
prophecy	a prediction of a future event
prophet	one who foretells the future, often inspired by the gods
pyre	a woodpile used for burning a body as part of a funeral rite
refuge	protection or shelter
seer	someone who foretells events
sorceress	a witch with supernatural powers
subdue	bring under control

transformed	changed in outward appearance
tribute	a payment made by one ruler or nation to another as an act of submission
Underworld	in Greek mythology, the world of the dead, ruled by the god Hades
vulnerable	capable of being wounded

PEGASUS
Zeus placed the winged horse among the stars. Only the front half of his body is shown.

ANDROMEDA
Andromeda was chained to a rock in the sea, threatened by a sea monster, and rescued by the hero Perseus.

CYGNUS
Cygnus the Swan is also known as the Northern Cross. Some mythographers claim the swan is Zeus in disguise.

LYRA
The lyre of the great musician Orpheus was placed among the stars by the Muses.

PERSEUS
The hero slayed the monster Medusa and rescued Andromeda from Cetus, a sea monster. He is shown holding Medusa's head.

HERACLES
Shown kneeling, holding a club, the great hero Heracles was turned into a constellation by Zeus.

Northern Hemisphere

URSA MAJOR
(Great Bear)
Callisto was turned into a bear and shot by Artemis. Zeus placed her among the stars, where she keeps an eye out for Orion, the hunter.

LEO
(Nemean Lion)
The lion of Nemea was slain by the hero Heracles as one of his twelve labors.

ORION

The famed hunter Orion boasted that he would kill every animal on Earth, so Gaea sent a scorpion to sting him. Zeus placed the hunter among the stars and the scorpion nearby *(continues from the Northern Hemisphere to the Southern Hemisphere)*.

CETUS

This sea monster was sent by Poseidon to punish Cassiopeia, the mother of Andromeda, for her vanity.

STARS OF GREEK MYTHOLOGY

Many constellations were named for characters in classical mythology. The practice of taking a being or an object and placing it among the stars is called *catasterism*.

SCORPIO

Sent by Gaea to sting the hunter Orion, the scorpion is placed near him in the sky to remind him of the consequences of boasting.

CENTAURUS

Centaurus represents the wise Centaur Chiron. Its brightest star, Alpha Centauri, is the closest star to the sun.

Southern Hemisphere

ARGO

The ancient constellation Argo Navis, named for the ship that carried Jason and the Argonauts, is made up of three smaller constellations: Puppis (the stern), Carina (the keel), and Vela (the sails).

HYDRA

The serpent was killed by Heracles as another of his twelve labors. In the sky, Hydra is the largest of the 88 constellations *(continues from the Northern Hemisphere to the Southern Hemisphere)*.

Note: Constellations in this illustration may not be exactly where they appear in the sky. For more accurate charts, go to: www.astronomy.com

FURTHER READING

Bolton, Lesley. *The Everything Classical Mythology Book*. Avon, MA: Adams Media, 2002.

Bulfinch, Thomas. *Bulfinch's Greek and Roman Mythology: The Age of Fable.* Mineola, NY: Dover Publications, 2000.

D'Aulaire, Ingri, and Edgar Parin D'Aulaire. *D'Aulaire's Book of Greek Myths.* New York: Random House, Delacorte Press, 1992.

Fleischman, Paul. *Dateline: Troy*. Cambridge, MA: Candlewick Press, 2006.

Hansen, William. *Classical Mythology: A Guide to the Mythical World of the Greeks and Romans*. New York: Oxford University Press, 2005.

Homer. *The Iliad*. Edited by E.V. Rieu. New York: Penguin Classics, 2003.

———. *The Odyssey.* Edited by Bernard Knox. New York: Penguin Classics, 2006.

Osborn, Kevin, and Dana L. Burgess. *The Complete Idiot's Guide to Classical Mythology*. 2nd ed. New York: Penguin, Alpha Books, 2004.

Roberts, Jennifer T., and Tracy Barrett. *The Ancient Greek World*. New York: Oxford University Press, 2004.

Sutcliff, Rosemary. *The Wanderings of Odysseus: The Story of the Odyssey*. New York: Random House, Laurel Leaf, 2005.

———. *Black Ships Before Troy*. London: Frances Lincoln, 2008.

WEB SITES

Encyclopedia Mythica: *http://pantheon.org/*
An online encyclopedia of mythology, folklore, and religion

Greek Mythology: *http://www.greekmythology.com/*
Contains information on gods, goddesses, beasts, and heroes as well as full text of selected books on Greek mythology and literature

Kidipede: Greek Myths: *http://www.historyforkids.org/learn/greeks/religion/greekrelig.htm*
Greek mythology pages of an online encyclopedia of history and science for middle-school students

Mythweb: *http://www.mythweb.com/*
An overview of the Olympians and selected heroes; includes teaching tips

Theoi Greek Mythology: *http://theoi.com/*
Profiles of the Greek gods and goddesses, and other characters from Greek mythology with an emphasis on their appearances in art and literature

INDEX

Marie O'Neill, Creative Director
Cheryl Clark, Editor in Chief
Caroline Anderson, Director of Photography
Cian O'Day, Ed Kasche, Jay Pastorello, Photo Research
SimonSays Design!, Book Production and Design

Illustrations:
Kevin Brimmer: 75
Paul Meisel: cover, 4–5, 7, 18, 96-97, 112-113, 117, 118–119, 121
G.F. Newland: 28-29
Rupert Van Wyk (Beehive Illustration): back cover, 33, 52-53, 76-77
Raphael Montoliu: 94
XNR Productions, Inc.: 118–119